Young People's
SCIENCE
Encyclopedia

Edited by the Staff of

NATIONAL COLLEGE OF EDUCATION

Evanston, Illinois

Volume 10/In-Ma

 CHILDRENS PRESS, CHICAGO

Photograph on pages 2 and 99: Saturn V rocket (NASA)
Photograph on pages 3 and 98: Aluminaut (Reynolds Metals Company)

Library of Congress Catalog Card Number: 67-17925
4 5 6 7 8 9 10 11 12 13 14 15 16 17 18 19 20 21 22 23 24 25   R   75 74 73 72 71

A dish radio telescope is used to search for and receive radio signals originating far out in space

Interstellar communication The term *interstellar communication* refers to any kind of message or signal that may pass between a STAR, PLANET, or GALAXY and the EARTH. Interstellar communication could refer to any communication between any star, planet or galaxy, and any other, except that our present limited knowledge must confine this discussion to the progress in communication between our earth and other heavenly bodies and systems that make up the universe.

. For centuries astronomers and other scientists have been trying to determine if there is intelligent life on other planets that might allow intercommunication with us human beings here on earth. These efforts have led to much speculation and educated guesswork. Our comic strips, television programs, and science-fiction stories have no hesitancy in relating earth contacts with outer space. Occasionally, it is reported that an unidentified flying object that has landed on earth has brought with it some creature or life form from another planet. But, thus far, these have been entirely without scientific proof or reality.

The greatest advancement in the exploration of interstellar communication has occurred since the relatively recent development of radio and radar techniques. Only by means of the seemingly limitless reach of the radio beam has it been feasible to send a signal to, or receive one from any

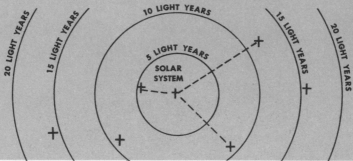

NAME OF STARS		DISTANCE IN LIGHT YEARS	
PROXIMA CENTAURI	MULTIPLE	4.2	TRANSMISSION COULD BE
ALPHA CENTAURI	SYSTEM	4.3	CONTINUAL FOR THIS MANY
SIRIUS (BINARY)		8.7	YEARS BEFORE RECEIVED IN THE
ROSS 248		10.2	VICINITY OF THESE STARS.

Radio signals sent to any of the nearest stars would take the distance time in Light Years to arrive there. Many single stars of the type which might have planets are many times farther. Signals such as Blip ... BlipBlip ... BlipBlipBlip ... BlipBlipBlipBlip are sent and listened for since the numerical sequence is thought to be the basic evidence of intelligence upon which an entire means of communication can be built.

body out in space away from the earth.

Communication between the earth and any other celestial bodies presents problems peculiar to time and space. Although radio beams travel at the speed of light—186,000 miles a second—many of the stars, planets, or galaxies we wish to signal are several hundreds or thousands of LIGHT YEARS away. This means we cannot wait for the answer. However, we can receive signals from those distant bodies —signals that originated those many light years ago.

The real beginning of the science of interplanetary and interstellar communication was in 1957 when a new device, a *radio telescope,* was constructed and placed in service at the radio-astronomy center at Jodrell Bank, England. This consisted mainly of a parabolic reflecting dish 250 feet in diameter, to which radio antennae for receiving and sending radio signals were incorporated. This radio telescope was placed under the direction of Sir Bernard Lovell, a British astronomer of note. This large dish could be moved in elevation and in azimuth. Its reach and resolution far exceeded any optical telescope that had ever been used.

The role of the radio telescope is manifold. It receives and sends radio and radar signals, or *blips,* between the earth and any kind of outer space object; it tracks man-made satellites, rockets, and space vehicles that travel beyond the earth's atmosphere; and, it reaches thousands and thousands of light years away to pick up signals, or, more accurately, electronic wave emanations, from stars or galaxies in the most remote constellations.

The first radio telescope at Jodrell Bank soon proved its capability as a practical tracking instrument when it followed Sputnik I, the first orbital vehicle to be placed into space by the Soviet in October, 1957. Soon after, the "big dish" at Jodrell Bank followed the course of the United States' first orbiting satellite, Explorer I, in January, 1958. This telescope has been used in the tracking of all future space vehicles.

The potential of the radio telescope was recognized immediately, and by 1967 there were more than 70 such reflecting dishes in operation or under construction throughout the world. The first one in the United States was a 140-foot diameter fully steerable radio telescope at Green Bank, West Virginia, built in 1958, and followed by a larger one there in 1965. The largest of them all is the 1,000-foot diameter radio telescope, located at Arecibo, Puerto Rico. This immense dish is located in a natural valley. Although the main bowl is not steerable, it has a reflector within the large paraboloid that may be directionalized. One of the most sophisticated of the United States' radio telescopes is at the Goldstone Space Communications Station, located in the Mojave Desert near Barstow, California. This 210-foot dish can pick up the most minute signals from satellites deep in space, and can bounce a radio blip from a star one hundred million miles away. When Pioneer VI went on its 200-million mile trip to Venus, and on to orbit the sun, the Goldstone dish received power signals no stronger than a trillion billionth of one billionth of a watt.

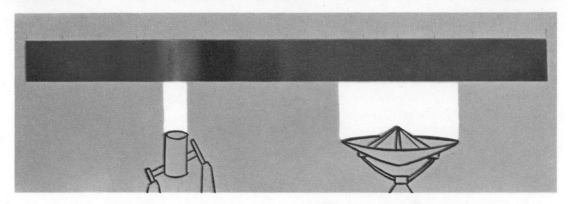

An optical telescope cannot "see" as much as a radio telescope can. The first receives only the narrow band of visible light, but the second receives the wider band of radio waves

It is well known that cosmic rays of the X-ray type emanate from stars and galaxies in constellations that are thousands and thousands of light years away. One of the most spectacular of these sources of cosmic ray emissions that has been identified by radio astronomy is designated as 3C273. Removed millions of light years from our earth, 3C273 has a luminosity more than one trillion times that of our sun. It is calculated that the diameter of this source of cosmic ray emission is equal to three light years.

International cooperation was demonstrated when the radio telescope at Jodrell Bank picked up the radio signals from Russia's Venus probe in 1967, and sent the data of Venus' atmosphere to all the world.

As an astronomical instrument, radio telescopes have the very desirable qualities of sensitivity and resolution. Sensitivity permits observation of the faintest and most distant phenomena, even though they may be a billion light years distant. Resolution enables the radio astronomer to separate one object from another, and to map the features of a space object. The National Science Foundation has said that the present radio telescopes reveal the "boundedness" of the universe, which constitutes the most fundamental measurement in the determination of our cosmology.   H. P. O.

SEE ALSO: SOLAR SYSTEM, SPACE

Intestine see Digestive system

Intravenous Intravenous means within a vein or veins. In intravenous injections, liquids, such as vaccine or saline solution, are injected directly into the vein.

SEE: INJECTION, TRANSFUSION

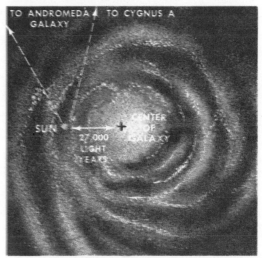

The enormous size of outer space can be seen when the location of the sun is pinpointed within its galaxy. But beyond this one galaxy there are probably many more. A radio telescope can bridge such distances

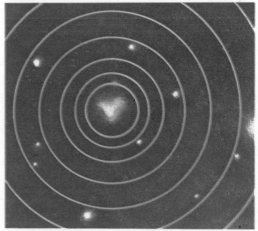

The most powerful source of radio waves so far discovered by scientists on the earth is Cygnus A galaxy

Intrusion In geology an intrusion refers to an *igneous* rock formation beneath the earth's surface. Intrusions occur when molten rock, called MAGMA, cools and becomes solid.

There are four kinds of intrusions, identified by their shape and position. *Batholiths* are the result of vast "lakes" of molten rock being pushed toward the earth's surface. They harden into broad masses. *Dikes* form when magma is forced upward leaving cracks or fissures through rock layers where it hardens. The formation's appearance suggests a dam or dike, and they are thus named. *Sills* form from magma hardened between layers of other rock. The horizontal appearance suggestive of window sills or door sills leads to the name. A thicker dome-shaped intrusion with a flat bottom is called *laccolith*.   D. J. I.

SEE ALSO: GEOLOGY, ROCK

Invention An invention is something new which has been thought up or developed by experiment. Airplanes, telephones, light bulbs, wheelbarrows, and shovels are inventions. An invention is distinct from a *discovery,* which is the finding of something that has long existed but has not been known before.

SEE: RESEARCH, SCIENTIFIC METHOD

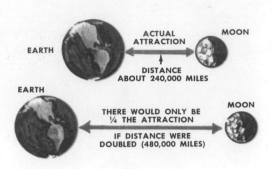

Inverse-square law The inverse-square law applies to many kinds of happenings involving space.

The force of gravitational pull between the earth and the moon depends upon distance. If these bodies were twice (two times) as far apart as they are, they would be attracted to one another less, but not one-half less. Instead the pull would be one-fourth. The pull varies *inversely,* a greater distance causing less force. The *square* of the amount (the amount times itself) that the distance changes is important.

For example, a one-ton weight is resting

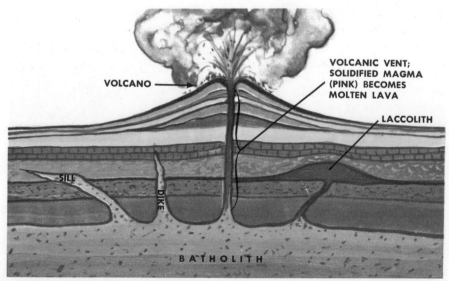

There are four types of intrusions, identified by their shape and position on the earth's surface. The center of the earth is the source of the pull, so while resting on the surface of Earth, the weight is at a distance of 4000 miles from the earth's center. Doubling the distance to 8000 miles, the weight's pull to Earth is $\frac{1}{4}$ ton.

Sound, light and other radiation follow this law. The amount of light reaching a surface five times as far away as another surface is the fraction one/twenty-fifth of that which reaches the closer surface.

Astronomers use this rule to measure distances to stars. Of two stars which are alike, only the distance to one can be established mathematically using angles. The other sends only $\frac{1}{64}$ as much light as the first, but its angle is too small to measure. If the first star is 20 light years away, the second will be eight times as far.

A person standing 100 feet from a radioactive source receives a certain amount of radiation. If he moves closer, to 50 feet, one/half the distance, he gets four times as much. F. R. W.

SEE ALSO: LIGHT

Invertebrate (inn-VER-tuh-brate) An invertebrate is any animal not possessing a spinal column or notochord (the forerunner of the spinal column). All members of the animal kingdom except most of the Phylum CHORDATA are invertebrates.

SEE: ANIMALS, CLASSIFICATION OF

Involuntary muscle see Muscle system, Muscle tissue

Iodine (EYE-uh-dyne) Iodine is a non-metallic element belonging to the HALOGEN family. It was discovered in 1812 by B. Courtois. At room temperature, iodine is a black crystalline solid. When it is heated it turns to a deep violet gas.

Iodine occurs as iodide ion in animal and vegetable matter. It is abundant in SEAWEED. The THYROID gland needs iodides to make its hormone thyoxine. One common ANTISEPTIC is a 2% alcohol-iodide solution.

Iodine (symbol I) is ELEMENT number 53, with an atomic weight of 126.90 (126.91, O=16). V. B. I.

Ion (EYE-uhn) When an electron is pulled off a neutral atom, the particle which remains is a *positively charged ion*. Similarly, when an electron is added to a neutral atom the particle formed is negatively charged, a *negative ion,* because there is a surplus of negative electrons.

Ions are often formed in a chemical combination between metals and non-metals. A familiar example is table SALT, sodium chloride. When the silverish, soft metal, sodium, is placed in a container of green, irritating, gaseous chlorine, a violent reaction takes place. The resulting substance is a white, crystalline substance, sodium chloride. In this case a sodium atom gives up an electron to a chlorine atom. The sodium becomes a positive ion and the chlorine becomes a negative ion, which combine into table salt (NaCl).

$$2\ Na + Cl_2 \rightarrow 2\ (Na^+\ Cl^-) \rightarrow 2\ NaCl$$

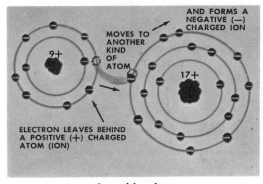

AND FORMS A NEGATIVE (—) CHARGED ION

MOVES TO ANOTHER KIND OF ATOM

ELECTRON LEAVES BEHIND A POSITIVE (+) CHARGED ATOM (ION)

A positive ion

There are differences between the properties of an ion and those of the corresponding neutral substance. For instance:

Chlorine, Cl_2

Greenish-yellow in color
Strong, irritating taste and odor (poison)
Combines readily with metals
Combines readily with hydrogen
Does not react with silver ion (Ag^+)
Very soluble in carbon tetrachloride

Chloride ion, Cl^-

Colorless
Mild, pleasant taste (as in table salt)
Does not react with metals
Does not react with hydrogen
Reacts with silver ion (Ag^+)
Not soluble in carbon tetrachloride

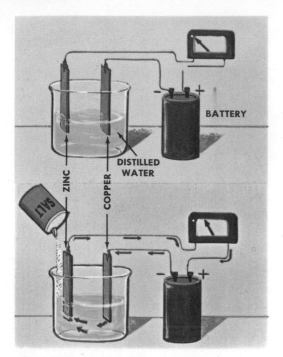

An ionized solution, called an *electrolytic* solution, will conduct electricity

PROPERTIES OF IONS

By properties of an ion chemists usually mean the properties of solutions in which the ion occurs.

A solution of a single kind of ion, alone, cannot be prepared. Positive and negative ions are always present together, so that the total number of charges of each sign is the same. But each ion gives its own characteristic properties to the solution. These properties can usually be recognized whenever they are not masked by other ions. For example, a property of copper ion, Cu^{++}, is its blue color in water. All solutions of this ion are blue, unless another ion is present which has a characteristic color. A characteristic of hydrogen ion, H^+ or H_3O^+, is its sour taste. Silver ion, Ag^+, shows the property of forming a white solid precipitate when mixed with solutions of chloride ion, Cl^-.

IONS IN SOLUTION

In 1887, Svante Arrhenius, a Swedish chemist, hypothesized that many substances exist in solutions as ions. Only one sort of experimental evidence suggested the existence of charged particles in solution, the evidence that the solution conducted ELEC-TRICITY. This could be shown by using a battery, a pair of electrodes, and a low voltage light bulb. If the solution conducts electricity the light bulb would light and ions must be present. If pure water is used the light bulb will not light. There are no ions in pure water. A solution which conducts electricity is called an *electrolytic solution*.

SOLUBILITY OF IONS

Many fluids in the human body consist largely of dilute solutions of ions. Some of the materials that plants manufacture into their food and man's enters their roots as ions dissolved in water. Rain water wears away solid rocks, in part because of its ability to dissolve their material as ions. The salt in sea water is dissolved as ions. J. R. S.
SEE ALSO: CHEMISTRY, ELECTROLYSIS, ELEMENTS, IONIZATION, SOLUTION

Ionization (eye-uhn-nuh-ZAY-shun) Ionization is the process of turning uncharged atoms or groups of atoms into *ions*. Ions carry an electric charge. This occurs when atoms either lose or gain electrons. With fewer electrons, the charge is positive. More electrons create a negative charge.

It is rather striking that after ionization most atoms have the same number of electrons as the inert gases (those that do not readily combine with others). The resistance to change (stability) of these ions and the chemical inactivity of the inert gases is attributed to a special electronic arrangement. These atoms, except for helium, have eight electrons in the outermost energy level. METALS, such as sodium, lose electrons readily, ionize, since they have one or two more electrons than the inert gases. Nonmetals such as chlorine, gain electrons easily in ionization since they have one or two fewer electrons than the corresponding inert gas. J. R. S.
SEE ALSO: ATOM, GAS, HYDROLYSIS, ION

Ionosphere see Atmosphere

Iridescence (ih-rih-DESS-uhns) Iridescence is the appearance of SPECTRUM colors on a colorless surface. Layers or irregularities in the surface cause some wave lengths of reflected white light to cancel each other out, leaving the complementary COLOR visible.
SEE: LIGHT

Iridium (ih-RIDD-ee-um) Iridium is an element with the chemical symbol Ir. It is a very heavy, hard, white, metallic element of the platinum group. Iridium is found in gravel deposits of California and Russia.

Iridium (Ir) is used as an alloying metal for hardening platinum. Platinum used in jewelry contains approximately 10% iridium. ALLOYS of OSMIUM and iridium are employed for fountain pen tips. Iridium alloys are also used in making hypodermic needles, other surgical instruments, watch and compass bearings, magneto-point contacts, and in photography.

Iridium has an atomic number of 77. Its atomic weight is 192.2.   P. F. D.

SEE ALSO: ELEMENTS, PLATINUM

Iris (plant) The stem of this plant is under the ground. Only the long slender leaves and flower stalk grow above the soil. Flowers may be blue, purple, yellow, or a grayish white. Irises are often called "flags."

This monocot gives its name to a whole group of plants, the Iridaceae family. The underground stem is a BULB or RHIZOME. Leaves have parallel venation. Each flower has three upright divisions (*standards*), three lower divisions (*falls*) and three branches between (*styles*). Many blooms have a beard or strip of hairs which guide insects down to the nectar. Irises must be cross-pollinated. A flower stalk may be a few inches to six feet high, depending on the variety. In the temperate zone most irises bloom in the middle of summer.

Enemies of this plant include leaf blight and rhizome rot caused by certain bacteria. Iris borer and aphids are also pests.   H. J. C.

Iris (visual) see Eye

Irish moss see Thallophytes

A common garden iris
F. A. Blashfield

Iron Iron is a silvery-white metal found in the earth's crust. It is never found in its pure state unless it comes from a meteorite. Iron is one of man's most used metals. Compounds of iron help sustain life, and are present in body cells of plants and animals, including human beings.

Primitive man first made use of iron mainly for tools and weapons. Iron was not the first METAL to be extracted from its ores. Copper proved much easier to smelt and process than iron, and was used earlier. The Egyptians were the first people to make extensive use of iron.

The earth's crust consists of about 5% iron. There is considerable evidence indicating that the interior of the earth consists of large amounts of iron. There are several large iron ore deposits in North America, principally in the states of Minnesota, New York, Alabama, and California, and in Canada.

The chemical symbol for iron is Fe. The ores of iron are found naturally as Fe_2O_3 (hematite), as Fe_3O_4 (magnetite), and as FeS_2 (pyrite). HEMATITE is found as black or gray crystals, and is usually located in its hydrate form, $2Fe_2O_3 3H_2O$, called *limonite*. MAGNETITE is a hard, black mineral, strongly magnetic. PYRITE is used in the chamber process for making sulfuric acid. Because of its sparkling yellow look, it is called "fool's gold."

For nearly 100 years, the great hematite deposits of iron ore in the Mesabi Range in Minnesota supplied much of the country's iron. However, these deposits began to run out in the early 1950s. Now the use of low-grade *taconite* ore has largely replaced ore from the Mesabi deposits. Taconite, in pelletized lumps, is the most important kind of iron ore in the United States. It is now used in steelmaking.

Iron is a metallic element, with a mineral hardness in Group V; it has a specific gravity (density) of 7.86, and a specific heat of 11 calories per gram per degree centigrade. It melts at 1535° C., and boils at 2375° C. Iron's atomic number is 26, and its atomic weight is 55.847. It combines readily to form carbides,

Inland Steel

Iron ore is often obtained from an open pit mine

United States Steel

The ore is loaded and shipped to mills

Inland Steel

Varieties of iron ore

oxides, hydroxides, nitrides, nitrates, phosphides, phosphates, sulfides, and sulfates.

Iron ore, before smelting, is improved by a process known as *beneficiation*. Screening or crushing the ore and either oxidizing or reducing the ore by roasting improves the quality of the ore.

Iron ore is then taken to steel mills where the ore is reduced in large smokestack devices called *blast furnaces*. The furnaces are charged with measured amounts of ore, coke, and limestone. Hot air is forced into the bottom of the furnace to combine with the coke to form carbon monoxide. CARBON MONOXIDE is a good reducing agent and easily permeates the ore. The reaction involved here is

$$Fe_2O_3 + 3CO \rightarrow 2Fe + 3CO_2$$

Some of the iron combines with the carbon to form *iron carbide* (Fe_3C) or *cementite*. This substance is very important because it lowers the melting point of the iron about 400° C. The molten material is removed from the bottom of the furnace periodically and is cast into bars called *pig iron*. Limestone is added to the blast furnace to combine with the impurities which are in the form of silica, alumina, magnesia, and lime. The limestone and the

Pig iron ladle

Inland Steel

impurities form a fusible mass or *slag,* which is removed from the furnace from time to time. The reaction is

$$CaCO_3 + SiO_2 \rightarrow CaSiO_3 + CO_2.$$

About 10% of the pig iron produced is used for *cast iron.* The pig iron is melted in *foundries* and poured into sand molds to produce *castings.* There are many cast iron products, such as fire hydrants, automobile engine blocks, toys, and ship propellers. For many products, cast iron is the most economical material that can be used.

Wrought iron is also made of pig iron, using a silicate slag to make the iron malleable. Wrought iron is of high quality. It may be hammered and forged into a wide variety of shapes and products. The silica content gives wrought iron great resistance to rust and atmospheric corrosion. It is used architecturally for furniture and for pipe.   H. P. O.

SEE ALSO: ELEMENT, FOUNDING, STEEL

Iron lung Breathing is necessary for life. Certain diseases such as POLIO-MYELITIS can cause injury to the muscles of breathing so that normal breathing is impossible. In such an event it is necessary to life to maintain breathing by artificial means, such as with an *iron lung.*

The iron lung, or *Drinker Respirator* (named for the designer, Philip Drinker of Boston), was originated in 1928 to help maintain respiration for long periods of time.

The iron lung is a metal tank built to enclose all of the patient's body except the head. A rubber collar fits securely around the neck to prevent the escape of air from the machine. The machine operates to lower and to raise the AIR PRESSURE at alternating intervals within the tank. When the pressure is decreased, the chest expands and air is taken into the lungs. When the pressure is increased, the chest is compressed and air is forced out of the lungs.

These alternating changes in pressure are controlled by an electric device which forces air from the tank into a bag at the foot of the respirator. Pressure within the tank is decreased when the bag is filled. The pressure increases in the iron lung when the air is sucked from the bag into the machine.

There are portholes along the side of the iron lung through which the patient can be cared for.   G. A. D.

SEE ALSO: ARTIFICIAL RESPIRATION, RESPIRATORY SYSTEM

An iron lung maintains breathing by artificial means

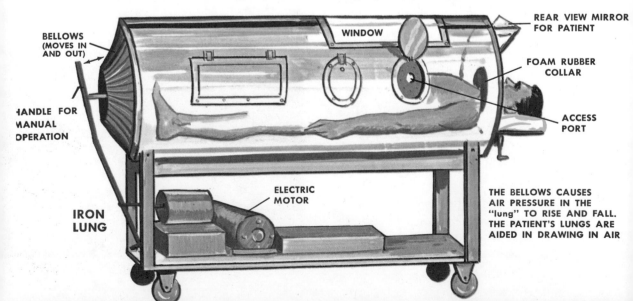

BELLOWS
(MOVES IN
AND OUT)

WINDOW

REAR VIEW MIRROR
FOR PATIENT

FOAM RUBBER
COLLAR

HANDLE FOR
MANUAL
OPERATION

ACCESS
PORT

ELECTRIC
MOTOR

IRON
LUNG

THE BELLOWS CAUSES
AIR PRESSURE IN THE
"lung" TO RISE AND FALL.
THE PATIENT'S LUNGS ARE
AIDED IN DRAWING IN AIR

Ironwood branch, fruit and wood

Ironwood It is the common name for blue beech and hop hornbeam. This tree grows 20 to 40 feet high. Bright green leaves turn to yellow in the fall. Bark is smooth and dark gray in color. Flowers and fruit grow in clusters.

The wood of the ironwood tree is very close-grained. It is one of the strongest, toughest, and heaviest woods used by man. However, the production of ironwood lumber is not too prevalent throughout the world, except in eastern North America. Simple leaves are egg-shaped and arranged alternately on branches. Leaf margins are doubly serrated. Male and female FLOWERS form inflorescences. Monoecious catkins appear in April. Each flower matures into a one-seeded nutlet. It is attached to leafy bracts. Ironwood is a member of the birch or Betulaceae family of dicots.   H. J. C.

SEE ALSO: HARDWOOD

Irradiation Irradiation is exposure to RADIOACTIVITY or to ultraviolet rays as a source of vitamins A and D. In optics, it is the enlargement of a bright object against a dark background.

Irrigation Irrigation is the watering of land by some means other than rainfall. There are many parts of the world that do not receive very much rainfall. Farmers in these areas cannot grow the crops that are needed to feed people who live there. In these places, irrigation is often used. This is only possible if there is water available nearby in the form of wells, rivers, lakes, or man-made reservoirs. There are many different ways in which the irrigation water may be brought to the fields and crops. If the slope of the land is right, small irrigation ditches may be dug from a main reservoir leading to the fields where they branch out. At other times, pumps must be used. Often a combination of pumps and sprinklers are used.

About 500,000 acres of land in the Imperial Valley of California, as well as in large parts of Utah, Arizona, New Mexico, and Texas, have been irrigated for years by bringing water from reservoirs, lakes and streams many miles away. In the state of Washington, the Grand Coulee Dam on the Columbia River has brought water to more than a million acres of otherwise arid land. Each year more arid land in the western United States is made into good farmland by irrigation. When the water is brought to the soil, the minerals and nutrients become available to the plants.

Fields of sugar beets, wheat, alfalfa, and other crops are grown in what were at one time DESERT regions of the West. Orange groves thrive where once only cacti could survive. There are some farms that branch out water from their own deep wells for irrigation. Irrigation is one way to supply water to plants that otherwise could not grow.   V. V. N.

SEE ALSO: DAM, DROUGHT

Farm irrigation may follow land contours
U. S. Department of Agriculture photo

Island An island is a body of land completely surrounded by water. At least a part of the land is always above the *high-water mark*. If this body of land surrounded by water is covered at high tide, it is not called an island but a *sandbank,* a *reef,* or a *shoal.*

In size, islands range from tiny ledges of rock peeping above the surface of the sea to huge land masses measuring hundreds of thousands of square miles in area. There are two basic classes of islands—continental and oceanic. *Continental* islands are bodies of land that were formerly joined to continents. These islands represent the unsubmerged portions of the continental shelves. *Oceanic* islands have been built up from the ocean bottoms by natural forces. They are usually located away from the shores of the nearest CONTINENT.

EROSION action by waves has caused the formation of some continental islands, while others have resulted from the submergence or sinking of coastal highlands. Only the high points of these highlands now remain above water. Other continental islands have been built from rock fragments as the result of wave erosion, or from deposits in the form of SANDBARS, or from outlying portions of a growing river DELTA.

It is not unusual for there to be only a shallow channel between a continent and an adjacent island that was once attached to it. For example, the English Channel is so shallow that England would again form part of the mainland if the level of the channel fell just a few hundred feet or if the floor rose by the same amount.

Islands found in the open ocean were formed in other ways. Many of these islands have been formed by the action of volcanoes on the floor of the ocean. Others have been formed by the growth of coral around the fringe of a volcanic peak that has submerged below sea level due to faulting or folding of the crust of the ocean floor. Some islands have formed as the result of the emergence of coastal areas.

A volcanic island grows by slow accretion of hardened lava

Many islands are the result of volcanic origin. As *magma* flows from deep within the crust of the ocean floor, the lava, cinders, and other volcanic debris build up one layer after another. Over the years, this crustal buildup is finally great enough so that the peak of the volcanic cone is above sea level. If the volcanic action continues, the island continues to grow.

Volcanic islands can be found in many dispersed areas of the Earth. Sometimes they occur singly, but in many cases they occur in chains. An example is the Hawaiian Islands, which consist of a chain of eight inhabited islands and a number of rocky islets. The larger islands represent the peaks of a submarine volcanic ridge, while some of the smaller islands of the group are classified as coral formations. V. V. N.

SEE ALSO: EARTH, OCEANOGRAPHY, RIVER, VOLCANO

Islets of Langerhans (LAHNG-er-hahns) The islets of Langerhans are groups of *cells* surrounded by a network of blood capillaries. They are scattered throughout an organ called the PANCREAS.

Insulin, the secretion of the islet cells, is not discharged or emptied through a duct. It is secreted directly into the blood. Because it enters the blood directly, it is called a *hormone* and the islet cells that secrete it are called *endocrine* organs. If the islet cells are unable to secrete INSULIN, the body cells cannot use and store sugar. This condition is called *diabetes mellitus*.

In the absence of insulin, sugar is no longer retained in the body tissues or in the liver. Sugar accumulated in the blood is removed by the kidneys and excreted in the urine. J. C. K.

SEE ALSO: DIABETES, ENDOCRINE GLANDS

Isobar (EYE-so-bar) Isobars are black lines on weather maps that connect points of equal barometric pressure.

Different elements having the same atomic mass number are also called *isobars*. Examples are: $^{14}_{7}N$ and $^{14}_{6}C$.

Isothermal lines Isothermal lines are drawn on a WEATHER MAP that show areas that have the same temperature at a certain time. Every place along a given isothermal line has the same temperature. These lines may show temperatures for a certain date and time or show averages over a longer period of time.

SEE ALSO: CLIMATE, TEMPERATURE, WEATHER FORECASTING

Isotonic solution (eye-suh-TAHN-ick) An isotonic solution has an *osmotic pressure* (the pressure of diffusion through a partly permeable membrane) equal to that of another solution taken as a standard. Medically, it is a fluid injected into the blood stream which is in osmotic equilibrium with plasma and red blood cells.

SEE: OSMOSIS, PERMEABILITY

Isotope (EYE-suh-tope) An atom, which is the smallest complete particle of an element, is composed of electrons, protons and neutrons. The number of electrons in an atom of a given element equals the number of protons.

This number does not change. The number of neutrons may vary. Whenever this happens, an element is said to exist in several forms known as isotopes.

For example, the HYDROGEN atom has one electron, one proton, and no neutrons. Deuterium, one of its isotopes, has one electron, one proton, and one neutron. Tritium, its other isotope, has one electron, one proton, and *two* neutrons. Iron has four *stable* isotopes, atomic mass numbers 54, 55, 56, 57, and 58. Yet each Fe (iron) atom has 26 electrons orbiting around the nucleus and 26 positively charged protons in the nucleus. The difference between the atomic mass numbers and the atomic number shows the number of neutrons in the nucleus *for each isotope,* namely: 54-26 or 28 neutrons; 55-26 or 29 neutrons; 56-26 or 30 neutrons; 57-26 or 31 neutrons; and 58-26 or 32 neutrons. Each isotope, thus, has a different number of neutrons. Each has all the chemical properties of iron.

A *radioisotope* is an element which disintegrates by itself. It gives off particles like helium nuclei (ALPHA RAYS) and ELECTRONS (BETA RAYS) and decays into another element. It also releases electromagnetic energy (GAMMA RAYS, LIGHT rays, X-RAYS). Some radioactive isotopes exist in nature $(^{238}_{92}U)$; some are manmade (synthetic ACTINIDE ELEMENTS, $^{60}_{27}Co$).

The emitted particles and energy can be detected and traced by a Geiger-Müller counter or other radiation detection instruments. Thus, in industry, radioactive isotopes can be used to trace materials, measure thicknesses and flaws, sterilize food, and give heat and power.   M. S. P.

SEE ALSO: ELEMENTS, NUCLEAR ENERGY, NUCLEAR SCIENCE, RADIATION

NUCLEAR REACTOR-PRODUCED RADIOISOTOPES

These elements have been bombarded by neutrons, some of which became part of the nucleus. As nuclear balance is reached, radiation is emitted as beta or gamma rays. New elements are the final product. (MeV = one million electron volts.)

ELEMENT	ISOTOPE	HALF-LIFE	MAXIMUM ENERGY OF RADIATION	
			BETA	GAMMA
CARBON	C^{14}	5770 years	0.156 MeV	—
SODIUM	Na^{24}	14.9 hours	1.39	2.753 MeV
CALCIUM	Ca^{45}	164 days	0.25	—
IRON	Fe^{59}	45.1 days	0.46, 0.27	1.10, 1.29
COBALT	Co^{60}	5.3 years	0.31	1.17, 1.33
STRONTIUM	Sr^{90}	28 years	0.54	—
IODINE	I^{131}	8.05 days	0.61	0.36
GOLD	Au^{198}	64.8 hours	0.96	0.41

Isthmus (ISS-muhs) When two larger bodies of land, such as continents, are connected by a long, narrow neck of land, the connecting strip is called an isthmus. North America is joined to South America by the Isthmus of Panama. Sometimes peninsulas are connected to larger land bodies by isthmuses. Denmark is joined to Germany by an isthmus.

A canal through an isthmus connects larger bodies of water. The Panama Canal, cutting through the Isthmus of Panama, saves a ship going from the Atlantic to the Pacific Ocean a long and frequently dangerous trip around South America.

Many other famous isthmuses have historical and economic importance to the countries surrounding them. The famous Isthmus of Corinth joins the Greek mainland with southern Greece. Nova Scotia is connected to New Brunswick and to the mainland of North America by an isthmus. The Isthmus of Suez connects Africa and Asia. In Asia, the Isthmus of Kra links Thailand and the Malay Peninsula. C. L. K.

SEE ALSO: CANAL, OCEAN

Itch mite see Mite

Ivory Ivory is a type of tooth dentine present in the tusks of certain animals. It is harder than BONE. Its chief source is ELEPHANT tusks. Ivory products include piano keys, chessmen and carved ornaments.

SEE: TEETH, TUSK

An important source of ivory for delicately carved objects is elephant tusks

Isthmus of Panama

Ivy This is a common name given to a number of vines. English ivy is the true one since it was the first to be called ivy. The leaves of ivy are lobed and evergreen. Green to white flowers grow in clusters. The fruit is a black berry. It belongs to the family Araliaceae.

American ivy has five leaves. Green FLOWERS form an inflorescence, followed by dark, blue berries. Boston ivy is also called Japanese ivy. It has lobed leaves and a berry-like fruit. These two ivies belong to the grape or Vitaceae family.

Kenilworth ivy has irregular purple and yellow flowers which develop into a many-seeded pod. This herbaceous perennial has five-lobed leaves. It is a member of the figwort or Scrophulariaceae family.

Germany ivy has delicate climbing stems and yellow flower heads. This house plant is in the Compositae family.

Ground ivy has a trailing stem which takes root at intervals. Flowers are light purple in color. It belongs to family Labiatae. It is sometimes called Creeping Charlie. H. J. C.

An ivy plant gradually sends off shoots and can cover a large area

Jade plant

Jackal A jackal is a wild member of the dog family. It lives in wild areas and near villages of Africa and Asia. It roams in a pack, traveling at night, looking for carrion (dead animals) and garbage. A jackal will also eat plant parts.

The jackal looks somewhat like a small wolf. It is about two and one-half feet long with a tail like a fox's. Most jackals are yellowish brown, though other species are blacker or redder. They are easily tamed and bred to domesticated dogs.   J. F. B.

Jackass see Donkey

Jack-in-the-pulpit see Wild flowers

Jacob's ladder see Wild flowers

Jade (mineral) Jade is a tough, hard green MINERAL used for ornaments and jewelry. The Chinese prized it above all rare stones and metals. Early Mexican Indians used jade, believing that it could cure illness and disease. Bells of jade produce a clear tone.

There are two true jades: *nephrite,* which polishes to an oily luster, and *jadeite,* (most prized) which polishes to a glassy luster. Quality is judged by the translucency, resonance, and color, which includes black, brown, green, lilac, and white. Highest GEM quality jade is translucent, emerald green jadeite.   D. J. I.

SEE ALSO: MINERALOGY

Green jade

Jade (plant) The jade is a plant with thick, fleshy, green leaves. The leaves often have unusual shapes. Jade is cultivated as a GREENHOUSE or pot plant because of its interesting leaves.

The jade plant has small flowers that are usually white, rose-pink, or yellow. It rarely blooms as a house plant but is otherwise quite hardy unless over-watered. It has a dry fruit. It is at its best when raised in the greenhouse.   M. R. L.

Jaguar see Cat family

Japanese beetle see Insecta

Japonica see Camellia

Jasmine shrub

Jasmine The jasmines are shrubs and vines belonging to the OLIVE family. These plants are raised for their beautiful and fragrant flowers. The flowers are usually yellow or white. They grow in clusters. Jasmines are tropical or subtropical plants. Most of them originated in Eurasia and Africa. It is also called *jessamine.*

Jasper see Quartz

Atlantic jellyfish

Buchsbaum

Jaundice (JAWN-diss) Jaundice is indicated when the color of the skin becomes yellowish. In this condition the BILE pigments of the BLOOD are increased, thus staining the skin and all the tissues. This discoloration may also come from a breaking up of the coloring matter of the blood.

Jaundice is not a disease. It is a symptom found in several diseases. It is commonly seen in *hepatitis* which is an inflammation of the liver. HEPATITIS used to be called *jaundice*. H. K. S.

SEE ALSO: DIGESTIVE SYSTEM, LIVER

Java man see Evolution of man

Jaw see Digestive system, Mandible, Skeleton, Teeth

Jay see Blue jay, Crow

Jejunum see Digestive system

Jellyfish Jellyfish are simple, transparent sea animals, varying in size from an inch to over ten feet. They have no backbone or skeleton and thus are not actually fish at all. The bodies are soft and often umbrella-shaped with stinging TENTACLES around the edge, for getting food. Ocean swimmers sometimes receive severe stings from certain kinds of jellyfish.

Jellyfish are of the group (phylum) called *coelenterates*. Their bodies are of two layers only, the outer, or *ectoderm,* and inner, called *endoderm*. A jelly-like substance between gives the animal form—and name. The stinging cells (NEMATOCYSTS) paralyze small organisms and the tentacles

Hawaiian jellyfish

Buchsbaum

bring them into the jellyfish through a center opening. The animals propel themselves by squirting jets of water from this opening.

Jellyfish are actually the *medusa* stage in the life cycle of certain coelenterates. Medusae produce *polyps* (stationary forms) which produce free-swimming medusae, and so on. This may represent an animal form of alternation of generations.

Comb jellies and sea walnuts, of a group called *ctenophores,* are often called jellyfish. Their structure varies somewhat from coelenterates, and they are usually classified separately from coelenterates. They have glue-secreting cells on tentacles and comb plates of fused cilia for swimming. D. J. I.

SEE ALSO: COELENTERATA; CTENOPHORA; MAN-OF-WAR, PORTUGUESE

Jenner, Edward (1749-1823) Edward Jenner was an English physician who discovered a vaccine to prevent SMALLPOX. Smallpox is such a rare disease now that it is hard to realize that during the Middle Ages it was the cause of horrible epidemics throughout Europe. Not only was the death rate high, but those who lived through such epidemics were permanently scarred with ugly pockmarks. Many were left blind.

Jenner, the son of a minister, was born in Berkeley, England. After receiving his medical education under various teachers, he returned to Berkeley where he became interested in the popular belief that people who had had cowpox, a mild disease contracted from cattle, could not get the deadly smallpox. This was not always true, because, as he discovered, only one of the two types of cowpox could protect. He had a chance to actually test the belief when a dairymaid with cowpox came to him. He injected fluid from the cowpox pustules into a healthy, young boy. Two months later he injected smallpox fluid into the same boy who did not develop the dread disease. This achievement started a national VACCINE program which today is universal. The basic idea is used to protect against many diseases.   J. F. B.

Jerboa, a jumping rodent

Jerboa Jerboa is any of various fawn-colored, mouse-like, leaping rodents of North Africa and Asia. Though a relative of mice and rats, and about the size of a large RAT, it has long hind legs and leaps like a kangaroo.
SEE: RODENTIA

Jessamine see Jasmine

Jet see Gem, Mineral

Jet propulsion Jet propulsion is a source of great power used by aircraft and other vehicles. In nature, the squid draws water into its body and then rapidly forces it out to propel itself.

In a gas jet engine, air is drawn into the engine and is squeezed or compressed. Fuel is then sprayed into the air and the mixture is burned. The burning gases rush out of the rear of the engine and it moves forward.

Sir Isaac Newton's *third law of motion*, set forth in 1687, explains the movement of both the squid and the jet engine. This law states *that for every action force there must be an equal but opposite reaction*. A simple example is stepping from a boat onto

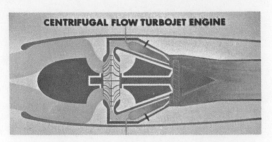

CENTRIFUGAL FLOW TURBOJET ENGINE

U.S. Air Force photo
Turbojet is the most common jet engine

a dock. The forward motion of your body is the action. The boat's movement away from the dock is the reaction. The reaction force is commonly called *thrust*.

Jet engines require huge amounts of air to operate efficiently.

The first jet propulsion device was Hero's Aeolipile built about 2,000 years ago. It consisted of a hollow sphere mounted on an axle with "L"-shaped nozzles attached. When it was heated, steam escaped through the nozzles, causing the sphere to rotate.

The simplest form of an aircraft jet engine is the *ram jet*. It is a specially shaped tube with no moving parts in which the ram air is slightly compressed. A kerosene fuel is added and the reaction of the burning gases results in forward thrust. The disadvantages of this engine and a similar type, the *pulse jet,* is that they must be accelerated to several hundred miles per hour by some other power source before they can be started.

The *gas turbine* or *turbojet* has become the more practical approach to jet propulsion. These engines have four basic sections —the *compressor,* combustion chambers, a turbine, and the exhaust section. Air is initially sucked into the engine by the rotation of the compressor blades, which act like a series of large fans. This air is compressed to as much as twelve times its normal free atmospheric pressure before it is forced into the combustion chambers. Fuel is sprayed into the dense air and the burning gases expand rapidly toward the open exhaust tail pipe, developing thrust. A turbine wheel is placed in the exhaust stream to absorb some of the energy to power the compressor. The turbine has blades or *buckets* which act like a windmill to turn the turbine shaft with the compressor attached at high speeds.

A *centrifugal flow* compressor was used by

early jet engines. Air was taken in at the center of a single impeller wheel and thrown to the edge of centrifugal force. This action compressed the air and forced it into the combustion chambers.

Almost all modern jet engines use an *axial flow* compressor which has a series of compressor wheels rotating between rows of fixed blades called *stators*. The air flow is parallel to the central shaft of the engine.

The power or thrust of a jet engine is measured in *pounds* rather than horsepower, which is used to rate the performance of a piston engine. The thrust of a jet varies with its speed through the air and the resultant ram air effect. A simple formula to convert thrust to an approximate horsepower rating is H.P. = (pounds thrust $\times$ air speed) $\div$ 375. Therefore, flying at 375 M.P.H. one pound of thrust would equal one horsepower. An *afterburner* section is sometimes added to the rear of a turbojet engine to provide for additional thrust for short periods. It is simply an extra long tail pipe in which additional fuel can be sprayed to take advantage of the unused oxygen in the exhaust stream. The afterburner is commonly used on military aircraft for take-off power and bursts of speed.

When a propeller is added to a turbojet engine, it is called *turboprop*. A specially designed turbine wheel absorbs the maximum energy from the exhaust gases to drive the propeller, in addition to the compressor and engine accessories. In this engine, the propeller provides the main propulsive force with only about ten percent of the thrust coming from the jet action.

Another variation of the turbojet is the more advanced *turbofan* engine. A large ducted fan is added to the front or rear of the basic engine and is connected to an additional turbine placed in the main exhaust system. The fan accelerates large quantities of cold

The ramjet depends on the ram effect, compression of air through a small opening

U.S. Air Force photo

RAM JET ENGINE

✳ **THINGS TO DO**

PRINCIPLE OF JET PROPULSION: EVERY ACTION PRODUCES AN EQUAL AND OPPOSITE REACTION

1　Stand in a wagon which holds a number of bricks. Throw one brick out. This starts the wagon rolling in the opposite direction.
2　As you throw each brick out, motion is added to the wagon. Note that the last brick thrown out adds more motion than the earlier ones. This happens because the wagon is lighter.
3　A heavy fuel-laden rocket barely moves. But as the pushing force acts on the lightening rocket, it accelerates until the fuel is exhausted or turned off.

air, which bypasses the main engine to gain as much as a thirty-five percent increase in thrust. This also permits a decrease in fuel consumption.

Huge advanced design jet engines for the supersonic transport (SST) are now in the testing stage. These 60,000-pound thrust power plants are nearly six feet in diameter and twenty-five feet long. The SST will be able to travel much faster than the speed of sound.　　　　　R. J. J.

SEE ALSO: AVIATION: ENGINE: FLIGHT, PRINCIPLES OF

The jet streams can aid pilots

Jet stream Jet streams are very fast winds high over the earth. They move like rivers of air, often as fast as 230 miles per hour.

The jet stream may be from 100 to 400 miles wide. It is 3000 to 7000 feet thick. It flows from west to east at about 35,000 feet above the ground.

Jet streams were first discovered by pilots during World War II. They found themselves seriously slowed down by these high winds. Now, jet pilots take advantage of jet streams in planning their flights. By flying with them, aircraft fly much faster over the ground.

Because the jet stream moves so much faster than the air around it, it disturbs the surrounding air and causes turbulence. This turbulence becomes less violent toward the middle of the stream.

As the seasons change, the jet streams move. In the United States they are usually farther north in the summer time than in the winter. They flow generally from west to east at all times of the year.   R. J. J.
SEE ALSO: ATMOSPHERE, WIND

Jewelweed see Touch-me-not

Jimson weed see Wild flowers

Joints Joints are cracks and breaks found within the bedrock that makes up the outer crust of the earth. As pressure and great strain is placed on this bedrock, *jointing* occurs. Some types of bedrock will have more joints than others due to their structure.

The area where jointing takes place is called the *zone of fracture*. This zone extends from the top of the bedrock down to a depth of a few miles.   H. S. G.
SEE ALSO: GEOLOGY

Joints, skeletal Whether at work or at play, man almost always moves some part of his body. Arms, hands, legs and feet may be in motion. All of these movements are possible because most of the bones of the body are movable. They are connected to one another in some way. The points of connection between the bones are called *joints*.

There are certain bones of human bodies which have little or no need for movement. For example, the bones of the skull are fixed and immovable. They are joined so closely by fibrous tissues that the connections between them appear only as lines. Such joints are called *synarthroses*. There are other bone junctions which provide for limited movement (*amphiarthroses*). An example of these connections is the so-called *pubic symphysis*. The pubic bones are in the lower front part of the ABDOMEN near the genital region. These two bones are held together by bundles of thick fibers called *ligaments*. During PREGNANCY there is a relaxation of these connections in the female body which serves as a preparation for childbirth.

Those joints which move most freely (*diarthroses*) are usually classified as hinge, pivot, or ball-and-socket joints. The *hinge* joints allow backward and forward motion in one plane. The bending of the elbow, the knee and the fingers are examples of motion provided by hinge joints.

The *pivot* joints allow for a rotating type of motion. For example the forearm can be moved in such a way that it seems to twist around itself. The head also moves in a rotating motion.

The connection between the thigh and the hip and between the shoulder and the arm provide good examples of the *ball-and-socket* joints. In such cases the head of one bone which is ball-shaped fits into a cavity of the other bone. Joints of this type provide the greatest freedom of movement. Usually the freely-moveable joints are held together by a capsule. The outer region is made of thick fibrous material and the inner part is lined by some special tissue called *synovial membrane* which secretes a thick, sticky fluid called *synovial fluid*. This fluid provides lubrication for the joints.

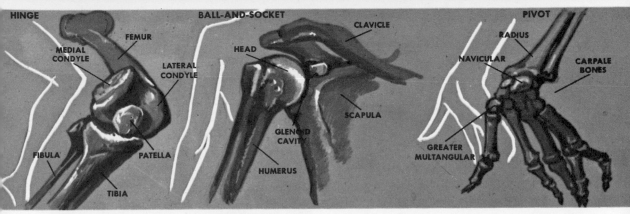

HINGE — BALL-AND-SOCKET — PIVOT

MEDIAL CONDYLE • FEMUR • LATERAL CONDYLE • HEAD • CLAVICLE • NAVICULAR • RADIUS • CARPALE BONES • GREATER MULTANGULAR • GLENOID CAVITY • SCAPULA • HUMERUS • PATELLA • FIBULA • TIBIA

There are basic types of movable joints in the human body. Each has a particular purpose and allows various parts of the body to move in a smooth manner. The movement of joints is controlled by the central nervous system.

In joints where tendons slide over bones or ligaments, small fluid-filled sacs, called bursae, prevent friction. The inner linings of bursae secrete the fluid (synovial). G. A. D.
SEE ALSO: ANIMAL, ARTHROPODA, BONE, FIBROUS TISSUE, MUSCLE SYSTEM, SKELETON

Jonquil see Narcissus

Joshua (JAHSH-you-uh) The joshua tree is a branched, tree-like yucca plant. It is found in the southwestern part of the United States. Yuccas are shrubs of the LILY family and all are native to desert regions. The joshua tree may grow to be twenty-five feet high. It has short leaves and clustered, greenish-white, bell-shaped flowers. The female yucca moth spreads the pollen of this flower.

Although most species of the yucca are low shrubs, the joshua has become a large, picturesque tree. The Joshua Tree National Monument in California contains important collections of yucca trees and other rare desert plants. J. K. K.
SEE ALSO: YUCCA

The joshua tree has tough spines

Buchsbaum

Joule (JOWL) A joule (abbreviated J) is a unit of energy or WORK equal to: (1) 10,000,000 ergs, (2) the amount of energy used in one second by an electric current of one ampere at a resistance of one ohm, (3) 0.738 FOOT-POUND, or (4) the work done by a force of one newton when the place where this force is applied is moved one meter in the direction of the force.

Joule, James Prescott (JOWL) (1818-1899) James Joule was an English brewer whose hobby was physics. His name was given to a unit of energy, the *joule,* and to a law showing how much heat is developed by a given electric current in a circuit.

Joule had no formal scientific training, but he did work for a short time under JOHN DALTON. In spite of his meager schooling, he was able to make important scientific advances because he realized very early the absolute necessity for accurate measurement and exact data.

Experts feel that James Joule did more than any other scientist to establish the basic theories of ENERGY. He also proved that heat is a form of energy. He showed that when work is done by a machine or electric current, an amount of energy is released equal to the amount of work done. Thus a joule is a unit of work or energy, a unit equal to ten million *ergs*. It is approximately equal to 0.738 foot pound, or 0.24 small calorie. However, the joule is too small a unit of measure to use commercially. Consequently, *kilowatt-hours* — a larger unit of measure — has replaced the joule in common use. D. H. J.

Judas tree see Redbud

Jugular vein see Circulatory system

Jumping bean Jumping bean is the name given to the seeds of certain Central and South American shrubs. The LARVAE of a small gypsy moth spin their cocoons inside the seeds and cause the jumping movements.

Jumping mouse see Jerboa, Mouse

Junco (JUNG-koh) The junco is in the sparrow family and is often confused with sparrows. Juncos are smaller birds with slate gray rather than brown bodies. They also have white on the belly and outer tail feathers.

Kinds of juncos, other than the common slate gray, are hard to distinguish in the field because there are several subspecies that differ only slightly from one another. Western species often have darker heads and rusty brown backs. The white-winged junco is the only one with white wing bars. Juncos are seed eaters and build their nests on the ground or on fallen logs. J. C. K.

SEE ALSO: BIRD, FINCH

Junco is a snow bird

June bug see Insecta

Jungle Jungles are found in the rainy tropic climates where rainfall is heavy. Jungles occur mostly along the rivers and mountain slopes of rain forests. Thick tangles of vines and other plants cover the ground. Many kinds of trees grow in the jungle. It rains daily or almost every day, and it is always hot and humid. Jungles are found in Brazil along the Amazon River and in Central America along the coastal mountains in the east.

There are many different "layers" of life in the jungle. The plants and animals found on the jungle floor are not the same as those found in the tops of the jungle trees. On the dark, damp, and cool jungle floor grow tangled vines, huge ferns, and giant palms, similar to those which grew in prehistoric times. Very few flowers grow in the dim light. In the Amazon jungles ANTEATERS and ARMADILLOS thrive on the brown, red, and black ants which seem to be everywhere. There are more ants than any other living thing in the jungle. Animals such as tapirs, peccaries, jaguars, and SNAKES live in the lower level of the jungle.

From about twenty-five to seventy-five feet up from the jungle floor, among the branches of the many different kinds of tropical trees, are plants and animals well-suited to tree life. Lizards, jungle turkeys, tree-living anteaters, sloths, and kinkajous spend their entire lives up in the trees, eating the abundant insects and ants. Some sunlight shines through the branches of the trees, and the air is warm and humid. Butterflies may hover over gardens of flowers hanging in the air. Among these colorful air plants (epiphytes) are delicate ORCHIDS and bromeliads.

The top of the jungle, seventy-five to one-hundred feet up from the jungle floor, is hot and bright with sunlight. MONKEYS noisily play in the tops of the trees, and brilliantly colored tropical birds, such as parrots, macaws, and toucans, fly overhead.

Jungles are old. The South American jungle is over one hundred million years old. It and the other jungles remained when the rain forests in other parts of the world were destroyed by long periods of cold and dry weather. The jungle is like a museum, for in it may be found plants and animals similar to those which lived on Earth millions of years ago.

When the jungle and other parts of the rain forest are cleared for agriculture, the soils, as a rule, are not very fertile. The heavy rainfall seems to remove valuable food nutrients and the constant high temperatures prevent the accumulation of humus to enrich the soil. Na-

There is an enormous variety of plant and animal life in jungles. Jungles are usually found near the equator in rain belts

Tropical rain forest

tives, after using a cleared space for a few years, may abandon it and move on to another location which they clear. This shifting pattern of jungle farming is called *milpa agriculture*.

D. J. A.

SEE ALSO: ASIA; PLANTS, TROPICAL; SOUTH AMERICA

Juniper Junipers are a large group of EVERGREEN trees and shrubs. They belong to the pine family. Some junipers are bushy, others are low-growing, creeping, or spreading. Some are medium-sized trees and still others look like tall narrow columns. Juni-

pers are often planted in rock gardens or in beds near the foundation of a house. Taller junipers are often planted in groups to provide pleasing backgrounds or screens. The word *juniper* means "forever young."

Junipers usually have gray-green needle-shaped leaves. There are two kinds of juniper leaves. Needle-shaped leaves grow on young seedlings and on leading shoots. Scale-like leaves grow on twigs of older trees. They look like a braided cord and are called *whip-cord foliage*. Junipers are raised from seed. The seeds take from two to three years to sprout. When the seedlings are large and strong enough, they can be set out in the nursery or garden. M. R. L.

SEE ALSO: PINE

The juniper trees are evergreens

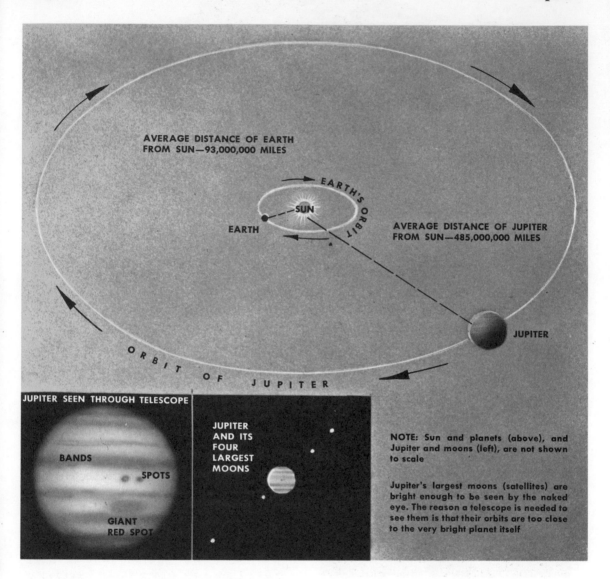

AVERAGE DISTANCE OF EARTH
FROM SUN—93,000,000 MILES

EARTH'S ORBIT

SUN

EARTH

AVERAGE DISTANCE OF JUPITER
FROM SUN—485,000,000 MILES

JUPITER

O R B I T   O F   J U P I T E R

JUPITER SEEN THROUGH TELESCOPE

BANDS

SPOTS

GIANT
RED SPOT

JUPITER
AND ITS
FOUR
LARGEST
MOONS

NOTE: Sun and planets (above), and
Jupiter and moons (left), are not shown
to scale

Jupiter's largest moons (satellites) are
bright enough to be seen by the naked
eye. The reason a telescope is needed to
see them is that their orbits are too close
to the very bright planet itself

Jupiter Jupiter is the largest planet in the SOLAR SYSTEM and is more massive than all of the others combined. It is brighter in our skies than any other planet except VENUS and (occasionally) MARS. It is more than five times as far from the sun as the earth is and it takes 12 earth years to revolve once around the sun. It is much too cold for any form of life we know to exist. It has 12 known satellite moons in all, the largest number for any planet. It may have other moons, as yet undiscovered. It can be seen without a telescope.

Of the four giant PLANETS, Jupiter is the nearest to the earth. When the EARTH and Jupiter are on the same side of the sun, Jupiter is about 369,000,000 miles from the earth. When Jupiter is on the opposite side of the sun from the Earth, it is about 600,000,000 miles from Earth. Jupiter's large orbit keeps the planet an average distance from the sun of about 485,000,000 miles. When Jupiter is on the Earth side of the sun, it is the second brightest planet.

It takes Jupiter almost twelve Earth years to make its journey around the sun. That means that the earth circles the sun nearly twelve times before Jupiter revolves around the sun once. Jupiter moves about 29,000 miles an hour. Jupiter's "year" is very long, but its day is very short. It spins completely about its own axis in less than ten hours. There are about 365 days in an Earth year. There are over 100,000 Jupiter days in a Jupiter year.

It is difficult to say exactly how fast Jupiter rotates because some parts of Jupiter spin faster than others. Jupiter seems to be divided into several wide bands. Those at the equator move fastest. Near the poles of Jupiter the belts take about five minutes longer to complete their rotation. The centrifugal force of Jupiter's high speed of ROTATION causes the equatorial belts to bulge, so Jupiter is not a perfect sphere. It looks like a ball that has been stepped on and flattened a little on top and bottom. Jupiter's diameter at the equator is about 88,770 miles. Between the poles the diameter is about 82,800 miles.

Seen with the naked eye, Jupiter looks like a very bright STAR. It does not generate its own light as a star does. Because it is a planet, the light is reflected light from the sun. Through a low-powered TELESCOPE Jupiter looks like a shining dot. Higher-powered telescopes show its polar flattening. Pictures made with very good telescopes show the bands of Jupiter. The bands are parallel to the equator and are of different colors.

Besides the colored bands, Jupiter has other markings that look like spots. Most of the bands and spots change colors and sometimes disappear for a while. The most famous spot of Jupiter is known as the *Giant Red Spot*. When it was first noticed, it was said to be a bright red, but it has faded now and looks brown. Sometimes it has casts of pink or salmon color. The spots of Jupiter have stirred the curiosity of scientists. Some scientists have suggested that the spots may be caused by violent storms or volcanoes. Others suppose the spots to be bodies floating in the gaseous atmosphere of Jupiter.

Jupiter would be a very inhospitable planet to visitors from Earth. Its temperature is lower than 200 degrees below zero on the FAHRENHEIT scale. Its GRAVITY is 2.6 times that on Earth, which would make a man weigh 2.6 times as much on Jupiter as he does on earth. The gravity of Jupiter would make walking or carrying nearly impossible. The atmosphere of the planet is believed to be made up largely of hydrogen, ammonia crystals, and deadly methane gas.

Jupiter is just a little more dense than water. Some theories suggest that Jupiter is a ball of liquid gas surrounded by a thick cloud of atmospheric gases. Another theory is that Jupiter has a core of rock or iron surrounded by a layer of ice that is over 17,000 miles thick. The ice is surrounded by a deep atmosphere of gases and crystals of ammonia.

GALILEO discovered the four largest of Jupiter's moons soon after the telescope was invented. Since then, eight more satellites of Jupiter have been discovered. Two of Jupiter's moons are about the size of the planet MERCURY. Three of them are larger than Earth's moon.

In recent years radio waves have been observed coming from Jupiter. The new science of radio-astronomy will probably reveal new information about Jupiter that optical telescopes have not been able to show.   C. L. K.

SEE ALSO: ASTRONOMY, RADIO TELESCOPE, SATELLITE, SOLAR SYSTEM, SUN

Jute Jute is one of the most useful fibers. It comes from one of two common species of jute plants. Jute plants are tall shrubs, from eight to fifteen feet high, and may be grown in any hot, humid climate. Most of the jute fiber comes from India.

The fiber which lies between the outer bark and the central wood of the jute plants is widely used. It is cheaply and simply cultivated, easily spun and dyed. Jute is used for burlap, webbing, twine, backing yarn for carpets and linoleum, oakum, paper, and heavy ropes.   J. K. K.

Fibers of the jute plant are used in many ways

Kaleidoscope (kuh-LYE-duh-skope) The kaleidoscope consists of a tube with an eyepiece at one end. Loose, colored particles between two glass disks are at the other end. Two MIRRORS are set at an angle of 60° running the length of the tube. When the particles are shaken, the mirrors reflect varying, symmetrical designs.

Kangaroo Some of these animals are the largest pouched mammals or MARSUPIALS. A full-grown male red one may be 7 feet tall and weigh 200 pounds.

When kangaroos move slowly, they are supported by a triangle consisting of the two front feet, the hind feet and the tail for balance. During rapid locomotion, which can be at speeds of 30 miles an hour in 25-foot leaps, it uses the hind feet alone, swinging the tail up and down as a counter-balance. The red kangaroo lives on the Australian plains, wallaroos live in mountains, and the gray lives in forests.

Hind feet of all kangaroos have the second and third toes fused together. These act

Kangaroos are marsupials

as a comb for cleaning the fur. Front feet can hold branches when the animal eats leaves.

Young embryos stay in the UTERUS for about two weeks. The PLACENTA rarely develops. One or sometimes two young are born in an immature state. They find their way to the pouch and become attached to nipples. After a few weeks, young leave the pouch but return for food and shelter.   J. C. K.

Kangaroo rat see Rat, Rodentia

Kaolin (KAY-uh-linn) Natural clay that is white or pale-colored and sand-free is called *kaolin* or *china clay*.

Kaolin is mined from powdery layers, the result of age-long weathering of FELDSPAR, chemically, an aluminum silicate. Most white dishware is made from shaped, oven-fired kaolin.

Abundant deposits of kaolin occur from Delaware to Florida and in Washington state. Commoner clays are less useful than kaolin because they occur mixed with sand and discoloring minerals.   D. A. B.

Kapok (KAY-pock) Kapok is a fluffy, silky, fibrous material that wraps the seeds in the pods or fruit of the *silk-cotton* or *ceiba* tree. This evergreen tree grows in many places in the orient. Its fibers are used as a filling for upholstered furniture, mattresses and life preservers.

The word *kapok* is a Malayan name for the tree. Most of the kapok used commercially comes from Java. The usefulness of kapok results from the physical properties of its fibers. They are poor conductors of heat, elastic, slow to absorb water, and buoyant because they contain many air-filled spaces. In the furniture industry, chemical foams are rapidly replacing kapok.   J. C. K.

Katydid see Arthropoda, Grasshopper

Kelp Kelp is the largest brown alga. It belongs in a group of plants that have no true roots, stems or leaves. A stalk or *stipe* is held to the bottom of the ocean by holdfast cells. At the other end are large blades called *thalli*. Kelp has chlorophyll; however, the brown pigment in the cells almost hides the green color.

Buchsbaum

Kelp

Kelps are in the division THALLOPHYTA. They are more complex than most ALGAE with some internal cells almost like vascular tissue. They exhibit ALTERNATION OF GENERATIONS with a very tiny gametophyte. Kelps remove iodine and potassium from the sea in great quantities. Man uses kelp for these products. The gelatin, *algin,* is also used.   H. J. C.

Kelvin, William Thomson, Lord

(1824-1907) Lord Kelvin was a Scottish physicist. He is known both for his basic research in various forms of energy, such as mechanics, heat, light, and sound, and for his inventions. His father was a mathematics professor at Glasgow University who gave all his children a good education. Both William and his older brother taught at the university when they were grown. William was knighted for his work on the Atlantic Cable.

Among his contributions to theory, the Second Law of THERMODYNAMICS (dissipation of energy) is best known. He devised the Kelvin TEMPERATURE SCALE. His studies also led to the development of modern refrigerators and freezers. He invented the mirror GALVANOMETER and a type of compass that was not disturbed by iron in a ship.

He was an exciting teacher who kept his classroom full of gadgets and demonstrated them during lectures. He often used his scientific friends as subjects for humorous demonstrations; but he was always willing to find practical uses for friends' discoveries and to promote their inventions.   D. A. B.

SEE ALSO: ABSOLUTE ZERO

Kepler, Johannes

Kepler, Johannes (1571-1630) Johannes Kepler was a German mathematician and astronomer of the late renaissance, who discovered the laws of planetary motion. SIR ISAAC NEWTON later used these laws as the basis of his Law of Universal Gravitation.

Kepler spent his entire life trying to answer this question: How do the bodies in the solar system maintain their positions? His firm belief in the order of the universe drove him to find a regularity in the universe. In finding that regularity, Kepler laid the foundation for scientific ASTRONOMY.

Johannes Kepler was born in Württemberg, Germany, and attended the University of Tübingen. At the age of twenty-three he became professor of astronomy at the University of Graz. Never a strong man, he suffered from the effects of a premature birth, and a severe case of smallpox at the age of four which left him almost blind.

At the University of Tübingen, Kepler studied the writings of COPERNICUS, and later at the University of Graz he wrote a book on how the heavenly bodies are kept in position in the solar system. This work came to the attention of Tycho Brahe, the famous Danish astronomer, who secured an appointment for Kepler as his assistant.

He used the theory developed by Copernicus that the sun is the center of the universe, a theory which was accepted at that time. However, according to this theory, orbits of the planets were circles. As Kepler studied Brahe's observation of the planet Mars, he realized that it travelled around the sun in an ellipse, with the sun at one focus of the ellipse, which the planet's ORBIT forms. This was the first of Kepler's three great laws of planetary motion. Next he proved that if a line could be drawn from the center of a planet to the center of the sun, as the planet revolved in its orbit, the line would sweep the same area in a given time. He also proved that the motion of the planet was fastest when it was nearest the sun, and slowest when it was farthest away. This was his second law.

Finally, using Brahe's data, Kepler announced his third law: The squares of the periods of revolution are proportional to the cubes of their average distances from the sun.   D. H. J.

Kerosene Kerosene is a colorless, oily liquid boiled off petroleum between 175°C and 300°C. Formerly it supplied FUEL for light, heat, and cooking, as well as fuel for tractors and farm machines. It is used as fuel for jet planes today.

Kestrel

Kestrel Though only twelve to fifteen inches long, the kestrel, a hawk-like, European FALCON, can spread its wings to twice its length and hover against the wind while it watches for small prey. The male has black-spotted, reddish plumage, with ash-gray crown and tail. The bird is also called a *windhover*.

Kid see Goat

Kidney The bloodstream brings waste to the kidneys. These take out everything from the blood except large PROTEIN molecules and blood cells. Useful substances such as sugar are returned to the blood. Wastes are kept and excreted in urine. Urine leaves the kidneys in tubes called *ureters*. These lead to the *bladder* where urine is stored until excreted. These organs form an EXCRETORY SYSTEM.

The kidneys are two bean-shaped organs on either side of the vertebral column and below the diaphragm (the sheet of muscle beneath the lung cavity). They are surrounded by loose CONNECTIVE TISSUE and masses of fat. The depressed concave side of the kidney

is called the *hilum*. At this point blood vessels and nerves enter and leave. The ureter also leaves from the hilum.

If a kidney is sliced in half, vertically, one can see the hilum expand into a cavity or *renal sinus*. The ureter expands into a funnel-shaped sac that projects into the sinus. The sac is called the *renal pelvis* and forms 3 cup-shaped tubes called *calyxes*. Calyxes branch to form 8 minor calyxes.

The kidney is composed of an outer cortex and an inner medulla. The medulla is lighter in color and contains cone-shaped striated masses of tissue called the *renal pyramids*. The narrow ends of the renal pyramids form *renal papillae* that project into the minor calyxes.

In the darker cortex, tissue appears granular and dips down into the medulla between

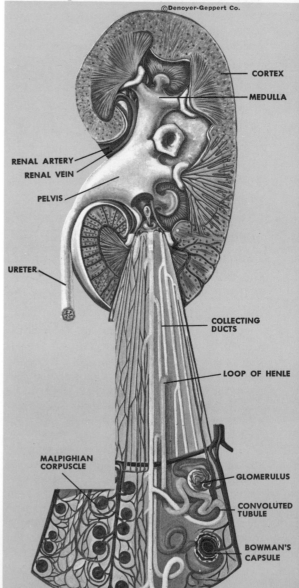

©Denoyer-Geppert Co.

CORTEX
MEDULLA
RENAL ARTERY
RENAL VEIN
PELVIS
URETER
COLLECTING DUCTS
LOOP OF HENLE
MALPIGHIAN CORPUSCLE
GLOMERULUS
CONVOLUTED TUBULE
BOWMAN'S CAPSULE

the pyramids. The parts extending into the medulla are the *renal columns*.

The unit of function in a kidney is a tubule called a *nephron*. The free end of the tubule consists of a double capsule (Bowman's capsule) surrounding a tuft of arterial capillaries (glomerulus). Capsule and capillaries together make up a *renal corpuscle*.

Renal corpuscles are connected to tubules that have three regions. A coiled region connected to the corpuscle, a long straight loop (Henle's) that dips into the medulla as part of the renal column, and another coiled section that connects to a *collecting duct*. Hundreds of nephrons empty into each collecting duct. Many collecting ducts join in a renal pyramid to form a papillary duct opening by a renal papilla into a minor calyx. There are 1 to 1½ million nephrons on each of the kidneys.

Reabsorption of useful substances back into the bloodstream, takes place in the tubular parts of the nephrons. Normally about 95% of the filtrate in the tubules is reabsorbed. Usually high-threshold substances (water, glucose) are completely reabsorbed. Low-threshold ones like *urea* (waste from proteins), some salts, and *uric acid* (waste from breakdown of purines found, for example, in RNA), are partly taken back. Non-threshold ones like creatinine (waste from muscle activity) or sulphates are not returned to the blood.   J. C. K.
SEE ALSO: NEPHRIDA

Killdeer These are noisy birds particularly when frightened. Their cry is a clear *"Killdee."* They have brown backs, orange rumps, white bellies, white bands between the eyes, white spots above them, and two breast bands.

Killdeer are a common PLOVER found in fields and pastures. They are larger than other plovers and are the only ones with double

Killdeer

breast bands. Killdeer are rapid runners and fly an irregular course. Usually they fly in flocks that break up while they feed upon insects and earthworms and sometimes on small crustaceans. Nests are built on the ground in shallow hollows sparsely lined with grass and pebbles. They lay four brownish eggs. J. C. K.

Killer whale see Whale

Kiln (KILL) A kiln is an oven or furnace which is used to heat a substance for the purpose of drying or hardening it. The term is commonly used to describe an oven used to heat ceramic materials to less than melting.

Kilo see Measurement

Kilocycle see Radio

Kilowatt hour The kilowatt hour (KWH) is a common unit for expressing a quantity of electrical energy. Electrical energy is measured by multiplying the rate at which electricity is used (POWER) by the length of time the electricity is being consumed.

The *watt* is a basic unit of power developed when one AMPERE flows at a pressure of one VOLT. Therefore, while the *watt-hour* is the basic unit of energy measure, the kilowatt hour (1000 times the watt-hour) is used for measuring the larger quantities of energy. For very small units of measure, the watt-second, also called the JOULE, is often employed.

$$\text{Kilowatt hours} = \frac{\text{volts} \times \text{amperes} \times \text{hours}}{1000}$$

E. I. D.
SEE ALSO: ELECTRICITY, WATT-HOUR METER

Kilowatt-hour meter see Watt-hour meter

Kindling temperature The kindling temperature is the lowest temperature at which a substance catches FIRE and continues to burn. A substance may have different kindling temperatures depending on the size of the particles into which it is divided.
SEE: COMBUSTION

Kinesthetic sense (kinn-uhs-THETT-ick) Kinesthetic sense is more commonly known as *muscle sense*. It is the automatic feeling a living being has which tells him the position of certain parts of his body or permits him to guess how much effort he must make to move or lift an object.

Every human being possesses this sense in varying degrees. Without it he would always need to use his eyes before he moved. For instance, to move the leg a person does not need to look at his leg, but if he lacked this kinesthetic sense, he would have to look at any part of the body before he moved it.

There are tiny sensory nerves which go from either the MUSCLE TISSUE, tendons, or joints up to the brain and act automatically without forcing one to think specifically about each movement he might make. This sense also tells a person the state of tension in the muscle, and helps a person control his movements or sustain them.

If one had a deficient amount of these impulses, he would not make the movements he had attempted. Through this sense a person also judges weight of objects. He can determine about how heavy something is before he tries to pick it up or move it and thus can prepare the muscles for the weight.

It is at the extremities that this sense is greatest. Fingers are more sensitive than wrists, and hands are more sensitive than forearms.   D. E. Z.

SEE ALSO: SENSE ORGANS

Kinetic energy see Energy

Kinetic theory (kih-NET-ick) The kinetic theory applies to liquids, gases, and solids. The explanation of the kinetic theory, however, is best illustrated in gases.

The kinetic theory assumes that all gases are made up of tiny particles called *molecules*. The distance separating the molecules from one another is very large compared to the size of the molecules themselves. The theory also assumes that the molecules are in a constant state of motion, except at ABSOLUTE ZERO. Because they are in motion, they collide with one another and with the walls of any container. The collisions

with the walls cause pressure to be exerted on the container. The molecules are assumed to be perfectly elastic so that when they collide, they rebound without any loss of ENERGY. The velocity of the molecules depends on the temperature. As the temperature increases, the velocity of the particles increases.   A. E. L.

SEE ALSO: BROWNIAN MOVEMENT, GAS, MOLECULAR THEORY, MOLECULES, PHYSICAL STATES AND CHANGES

King crab see Crab

King snake see Snakes

Kingfish Kingfish is a general name for a wide variety of food and game fish. Generally, the body is long, teeth are sharp and the snout is blunt. They have a single chin barbel. Their weight ranges from one to 100 pounds and their size from a few inches to six feet. The whiting, Sierra mackerel, white croaker and cero are kingfish.

Chicago Natural History Museum
King whiting, a kingfish

Kingfisher These birds occur in Canada and throughout the United States except in the southern area. Kingfishers are grayish-blue with white dots on the wings, white tipped feathers, white spots around the eyes, and a white neckband and belly with rusty streaks on each side. On its head is a ragged crest and it has a tail crossed with white bars.

Kingfishers live in wooded areas on the shores of ponds or streams. They perch on limbs hanging over the water and wait for prey. When they catch sight of a fish they

A female belted kingfisher

Swallow-tailed kite

hover over the water until time is ripe for a kill. Then with a quick dive, the kingfishers spear the fish with their sharp black beaks.

Most of the 800 species of these birds live in the Malay Archipelago. Only one genus, containing nine species, lives in America. All of these, except the belted kingfisher, live in tropical America.   J. C. K.

Kinglet The kinglet is any of several small songbirds. It is greenish with a gray breast and brightly-colored crown. The two North American species are the *golden-crowned* and the *ruby-crowned*. They live far north, but some are so sturdy they do not migrate to a warmer climate in winter.

Golden-crowned kinglet

Kite Kites belong to the hawk family and are birds of prey. Like hawks, they have slender pointed wings not built for soaring like the eagles. Old World kites are scavengers; American kites hunt living insects and reptiles. The everglade kite eats snails, prying out meat with its bill.

SEE: BIRDS OF PREY

Kiwi The smallest of the flightless birds are the kiwis. Because of dogs and pigs they are almost extinct. There are three species living in New Zealand. These are shy nocturnal (active at night) birds.

Kiwis are about the size of chickens. Feathers are long, hairy, and brown or gray. This type of feather may result from degeneration related to loss of flying ability. Bills are long and curved with nostrils on the tips. At night they smell and dig earthworms.

Kiwis weigh about 4 pounds but lay 1 pound eggs. One egg is incubated by the male for 25 to 80 days. Young are hatched feathered but take 3 to 4 years to mature.   J. C. K.
SEE ALSO: BIRDS, FLIGHTLESS: NOCTURNAL HABITS

Kiwi,
a flightless bird

Knee see Skeleton

Knot This is a pattern, often circles, found in wood. It begins when a young stem grows lateral branches. As a tree grows secondary tissue, the branch base gets buried in the trunk. Cells in the branch get hard from gums, resins, and tannins. Logitudinal sawing displays the cross sections of these branches.

Koalas live in trees

Koala (koh-AHL-uh) The koala bear is not really a bear, though its little fat body looks like one. It belongs with the other pouched animals (*marsupials*) of Australia.

The koala is about two feet long with thick, gray fur. It has a heavy body, no tail, large ears, a short snout, and cheek pouches for storing food. Its hands are split between the middle and index fingers, letting them grasp objects with a firm grip. They can climb trees and even swing between branches using their long, sharp claws.

The koala mother has one baby at a time. The early part of the offspring's life is spent in the pocket or pouch of its mother, where it nurses and hides. When the cub is older, it rides on the mother's back.

Koalas spend most of their lives in *eucalyptus* (blue gum) trees. They sleep during the day and eat only eucalyptus leaves and tender shoots at night. Koalas get water from the leaves they consume.   H. J. C.

Koch, Robert (KAWKH) (1843-1910) Robert Koch was a famous German physician and one of the greatest bacteriologists ever known. He discovered the germ which causes TUBERCULOSIS of the lungs. While on an official mission to Egypt and India, he also isolated the bacterium which causes Asiatic cholera. Koch spent eighteen months investigating SLEEPING SICKNESS among the people of East Africa and traveled to India as head of a commission to study bubonic plague. His investigations of the origin and treatment of MALARIA took him all over the world.

Robert Koch

In addition to these, Koch isolated the bacillus of anthrax, an infectious and generally fatal disease among cattle, and developed a method of inoculation to prevent the disease. He was internationally recognized as a pioneer in new methods of bacteriological research, primarily for isolating individual species.

Born in Klausthal, Hannover, Germany, this great man studied medicine at the University of Göttingen. When he was forty-two years old, he became a professor of medicine at the University of Berlin. The recipient of many awards and honors, he won the NOBEL PRIZE for medicine in 1905.   D. H. J.

SEE ALSO: BACTERIOLOGY

Kohlrabi (KOHL-rah-bee) Kohlrabi is a vegetable belonging to the CABBAGE family. It is a peculiar-looking plant because of its turnip-like stem which is edible. Actually, the stem looks like a bulb and may be six inches in diameter. A tuft of loose stems grows from this bulb-like stem. These smaller stems are eaten along with the main stem.

Kohlrabi

Kohlrabi was grown in Africa as long as 4,000 years ago. Today it is used for human and stock food, more in Europe than in America, and is sometimes found in home vegetable gardens. The taste and texture, except in very young plants, are not as pleasant as turnips or cabbage.   J. K. K.

Kon-Tiki (Kahn-TEEK-ee) Many centuries ago, the Inca Indians of Peru worshipped a sun-god whom they called *Viracocha*. Some scientists believe that this sun-god was called *Kon-Tiki* by people who lived in Peru before the Incas came. These people built many pyramids and huge stone statues, some of which are still standing. Long before the voyages of Columbus these fair-skinned people mysteriously disappeared.

Thor Heyerdahl, a Norwegian ethnologist, became convinced that these people, about 500 A.D., crossed the Pacific Ocean on balsa log rafts to escape from the Incas. They were, he believed, the true ancestors of the Polynesians. Could he also cross the ocean on a similar raft? Heyerdahl thought he could. If so, he would be producing some important anthropological evidence.

On April 28, 1947, Mr. Heyerdahl and five companions set out from Peru on just a balsa log raft which they named *Kon-Tiki*, in honor of the ancient sun-god. After 101 days of harrowing experiences, drifting with the Humboldt and South Equatorial Currents, they crossed 4300 nautical miles of

The Kon-Tiki expedition tested a hypothesis by direct experience, in crossing the Pacific Ocean on a balsa log raft

Pacific expanse, landing near the islands of Tahiti. This did not prove the theory, of course, though it strengthened it. But the voyage of these six intrepid sailors provided science with hundreds of valuable observations of the ocean and its creatures. R. N. J.
SEE ALSO: OCEANOGRAPHY

Kookaburra

Kookaburra (KOO-kuh-burr-uh) This odd bird is a KINGFISHER that does not eat fish. It lives mostly on crabs, mice, and reptiles, but also robs birds' nests of young nestlings. It is the largest bird in the kingfisher family.

The kookaburra is called the laughing jackass because it has a hyena-like laugh. These birds lack the brilliant colors of some of the tropical kingfishers. They have a mottled brown pattern all over their bodies, and their beaks are wider and shorter than the American kingfisher. They also lack the ragged head crest.   J. C. K.

Krypton (KRIPP-tahn) Krypton is one of the gaseous ELEMENTS. It is present in small amounts in the atmosphere, and in greater amounts in some volcanic gases.

Krypton was discovered in 1898 by two British scientists, William Ramsay and Morris Travers. They were measuring the densities of the trace gases from boiling liquid air, when they noticed a unique fraction of gas at density 3.71 grams per liter. Krypton is used in filling vacuum tubes and light bulbs, since its inertness keeps tube wires from oxidizing, just as other inert gases do.

Its chemical symbol is Kr; atomic number 36 and atomic weight 83.80.   D. A. B.

Kumquat see Citrus fruits

Laboratory A laboratory is a room or area devoted to experimenting or testing. It contains equipment necessary for research of all kinds.

School laboratories provide the facilities for doing basic experiments in CHEMISTRY, physics, and biology. In industrial laboratories, methods of production and testing are developed. Automobile, petroleum, and food production industries provide laboratories of this kind. In medical laboratories, examinations of blood and other body fluids and functions are made.

Testing laboratories, often private, examine and evaluate products for manufacturers, in order to improve their quality or develop new products.   D. J. I.

Laburnum (luh-BUR-nuhm) Laburnum is a genus of three trees of the pea family. The leaves grow in groups of three and the small yellow flowers are showy. Both leaves and flowers are poisonous. The delicately grained wood is used in making fine furniture. The trees grow best in the warm parts of Europe and Asia.

An ornamental laburnum

Labyrinth see Ear

Lacrimal gland see Eyes, Tears

Lactation see Mammalia

Lactic acid When the body becomes tired after running very fast, the tiredness, or fatigue, is due to lactic acid in the MUSCLES. This waste is removed by the bloodstream to the liver. In the liver it is changed to sugar or to glycogen, if it is to be stored in the liver or muscles.

Animal glycolysis is a process in which simple sugar and glycogen are changed to lactic acid and energy is given off. This occurs when oxygen is not readily available so that the body can continue to function. As the acid accumulates, some gets into the blood and its presence causes deeper and faster breathing. Part of the acid ($C_3H_6O_3$) is oxidized to CO_2, H_2O and O_2. Finally, the muscle and liver tissue can use this released energy to change lactic acid back to sugar.

Sour milk contains lactic acid produced by the lactic acid bacilli important in the fermentation processes.   H. J. C.

Lactogen (LACK-tuh-juhn) Lactogen is also called *prolactin*. It is secreted by the anterior or front lobe of the PITUITARY GLAND and may cause the milk glands to produce milk.

Now research seems to indicate that prolactin and the growth hormone STH may be the same substance or, perhaps, two hormones with similar effects. Prolactin is tested on pigeons. Young pigeons are fed crop milk consisting of sloughed-off lining cells of the crop. Injecting extracts of either prolactin or STH produces pigeon milk. Both of these hormones cause milk formation if injected into mammary glands. In rats, prolactin stimulates an empty follicle in the OVARY to become a secretory body (*corpus luteum*). Extracts of both the growth hormone and prolactin have the same action. Further physiological and chemical studies will be needed.   J. C. K.
SEE ALSO: MAMMALS, PREGNANCY

Lactose see Enzyme, Sugar

Ladybug see Beetle

Lady's slipper see Orchid

Laënnec, René (lay-NECK) (1781-1826)

Laënnec was a French physician who invented the STETHOSCOPE and who is called the "father of chest medicine."

Trained in medicine during the period when doctors learned about disease by examining human bodies after death, Laënnec was the first physician who listened to sounds in the lungs and hearts of his patients and then examined their bodies after death to determine the causes. He made careful observations of the wheezing, rattling, and whistling sounds and, to do this more skillfully, he invented the stethoscope, a simple wooden cylinder one foot in length. He conceived the idea from watching children use pins to scratch one end of a wooden beam while listening at the other end. Thus Laënnec was able to match the sounds, or symptoms, with the disease.

Born in Quimper, Brittany, Laënnec was sent at the age of seven to live with his uncle, who was the clergyman at the University of Nantes. When Laënnec was twenty years old, he went to Paris to study medicine. During his distinguished career he served as a physician at the Hospital Necker, professor at the College of France, and physician at the Charité Hospital. Laënnec was later to become gravely ill with a chest ailment, perhaps tuberculosis, from which he died in 1826. D. H. J.

Lagoon (luh-GOON)

A lagoon is a shallow pond or LAKE that is connected to the sea or another body of water by a small CHANNEL. The water is usually very quiet and peaceful because the channel is so small that storms and movements of sea water do not affect the water of the lagoon.

A shallow lagoon built by shore currents
Courtesy Society For Visual Education, Inc.

Lake

A lake is an inland body of still water that is not directly connected to the sea. Some lakes contain fresh water; others contain salty water. Most of the lakes in the Northern Hemisphere were formed by the glaciers of the Ice Age. If a river becomes blocked or is dammed up, a lake may form in the river valley. Some lakes are made by water collecting in the basins, or craters, of old volcanoes.

A lake may be formed by the blocking of a river valley due to a giant landslide, or by some other movement of the earth's crust. Ancient volcanoes may have craters that become filled with water, forming lakes. The source of water for a lake may be precipitation, rivers, and groundwater. Most lakes are in a state of balance; that is, they receive as much water as is lost through runoff and evaporation. In time, however, a lake will slowly dry up as silt and other minerals are washed into it by streams and are deposited on the lake bottom.

Glacial lakes are the most common type of lake in the Northern Hemisphere. As the ice sheets moved out of the north they gouged out areas of the land and in other places dammed river valleys. In still other places, they deposited large amounts of glacial debris. As the ice melted back, these areas were filled with water and became lakes. The glacial lakes found today were formed in recent geological time. The Great Lakes are examples of glacial lakes.

Barrier lakes, or lakes with no outlets, are found in various parts of the world. The Dead Sea in Asia and the Great Salt Lake in Utah have fresh-water inlets but no outlets. In these arid regions, water escapes from barrier lakes by evaporation. Salt and other minerals remain in the barrier lakes. Some such lakes are economically important because of the salt deposits that can be mined. Rivers may be blocked by silt deposits or land slides. This blocking causes a backing up of water, which ultimately results in the formation of a barrier lake.

Other lakes are created in regions with limestone bedrock. Rainwater dissolves underground lime rock and underground streams carry off the water. If the surface rock or earth above these caverns collapses, a basin is

Courtesy Society For Visual Education, Inc.

Crater Lake

Jean Lamarck

formed which may fill and make a lake. These lakes are called *sinkhole lakes*. They are common in southeastern United States.

Artificial lakes are becoming more and more common as new dams and super highways are constructed. These lakes are a man-made type of barrier lake. In some areas, abandoned stone quarries eventually fill with ground water and rainwater.   C. L. K.

SEE ALSO: EROSION, GLACIER, RIVER, WATER TABLE

Lake trout see Trout

Lamarck, Jean Baptiste Pierre (luh-MARK, ZHAHN bah-TEEST PYAIR) (1744-1829) Jean Lamarck was an outstanding French naturalist, best known for his theory of evolution and for the distinction he made between animals with backbones (vertebrates) and animals without backbones (invertebrates). It was Lamarck who invented the term *biology*.

While studying medicine in Paris, after having given up theology, Lamarck became interested in botany. He published a small book on French plants that brought him immediate recognition and membership in the French Academy of Sciences, but no money. Always poverty stricken, Lamarck gladly accepted the post of keeper of the herbarium at the Garden of the King, a post which paid very little but allowed time to study and read.

Although his position had been at the appointment of the king, Lamarck was not disturbed by the French Revolutionists. In fact, the new government accepted his suggestions of renaming the Garden of the King to the Garden of Plants, and to offer

courses there to interested young students. Lamarck was fifty years old at the time.

In the years to follow, Lamarck divided the animal kingdom into vertebrates and invertebrates. He developed a ladder of evolution beginning at the top with the vertebrates: mammals, then birds, reptiles, and fish. Among the invertebrates, he placed at the top mollusks, annelids (certain marine worms), radiates (starfish), and polyps. As he worked, Lamarck became positive that one life had developed from another. This was fifty years before DARWIN published his *Origin of the Species,* which further developed the idea with a different approach.

Lamarck also worked out a theory of ACQUIRED CHARACTERISTICS which states that the habits and ways of living of an animal cause inherited changes in its body form, its organs, and its qualities. When an organ is used, it develops; when it is not used, it disappears. As an example, he cited the giraffe, and he wrote: "We know that this tallest of mammals, living in arid localities, is obliged to· browse on the foliage of trees. It has resulted from this habit, maintained over a long period of time, that in all the individuals of the race the forelegs have become longer than the hinder ones, and that the neck is so elongated that it raises the head almost six meters (twenty feet) in height." Later scientists disproved this theory.

Lamarck died in virtual obscurity, but much of the work he did lived after him.
                    D. H. J.

SEE ALSO: EVOLUTION

Lamb see Sheep

Lamination see Plywood

Lamp A lamp is a device used to produce LIGHT. It uses either ELECTRICITY or the burning of oil, gas or other flammable materials.
SEE: BULB, ELECTRIC

Lampblack When an oil lamp burns, the soot, or unburned carbon, found upon the glass is lampblack. It is produced commercially in cast iron or brick furnaces, and is used in making paints, printer's ink, carbon paper and shoe polish.

Carbon black is similar to lampblack and is made by burning NATURAL GAS rather than petroleum oils or coal tars. It is important in the toughening of rubber. Because of its carbon content, carbon black is used in dry cells and radio resistors. THOMAS EDISON used soot from oil lamps in a carbon transmitter for the telephone.   J. M. C.
SEE ALSO: CARBON, COAL TAR

Lamprey (LAMM-pree) Lamprey eels are neither fish nor eels. They are long animals belonging to a group of jawless vertebrates (animals with backbones) with soft skeletons made of CARTILAGE. This group is called *Cyclostomata*. Lampreys are *ectoparasites*. This means that they feed attached to the outside of their victims—fish. They have funnel-shaped sucking mouths with hard, scale-like teeth that help them to hold on to their prey. A toothed tongue enables them to cut into flesh of the fish.

Lamprey and enlarged view of mouth

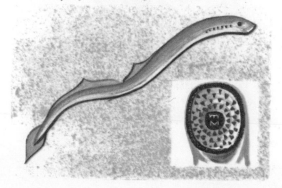

Lamprey eels live as adults in both fresh and salt water but all species breed in fresh water. They breathe by means of gills located in muscular pouches. The portion of the pharynx used for circulating water over gills is separated from the digestive tract. Thus the lamprey can feed and breathe at the same time. Unlike true fish, the paired fins and scales are lacking and there is only one nostril.

Lampreys have two semicircular canals for balancing organs rather than the three common to most vertebrates. The eyes are well developed and taste buds occur in the pharynx and on the surface of the head. Although a cerebral cortex can be recognized, the brain is primitive. The skull has no sides or roof.

The lamprey eels of the Great Lakes have caused great loss for the fresh-water fishing industry because the fish to which they have attached cannot be used.   J. C. K.
SEE ALSO: PARASITES, PISCES (ANIMAL)

Land, Edwin Herbert (1909-   ) Edwin Land is best known for his invention of the Polaroid Land camera. This CAMERA takes and prints a picture in ten to sixty seconds. The picture is printed on direct positive paper, using chemicals that are in the camera. The picture is then coated so that it will not fade. Special FILM which gives a negative also can be used.

Land also developed polaroid plastic which can filter glare from light. In 1959 he announced a new theory of COLOR vision: that the color of an object depends on a varying balance between longer and shorter wave lengths of light over the visual field. This may be useful for simpler methods of color televising.

Born in Bridgeport, Connecticut, Edwin Land studied at Harvard University. Many honors and awards have been bestowed upon him.   D. H. J.
SEE ALSO: PHOTOGRAPHY

Landslide see Avalanche

Langerhans, islets of see Islets of Langerhans

Langley, Samuel see Aviation

Lanolin (LANN-uh-linn) Lanolin is the grease found in the wool sheared from SHEEP. The grease or FAT is removed from the wool and later chemically "cleaned up" for use in pharmaceuticals and cosmetics.

Since lanolin cannot be dissolved in water, it is usually removed from the wool with a water insoluble SOLVENT. A good solvent for lanolin is CHLOROFORM, although it is expensive for this process. Lanolin is purified by a series of solvent extractions and may even be bleached to some degree to lighten its original dark color to a bright yellow. Lanolin is composed mostly of esters of fatty acids and a small amount of solid alcohols such as cholesterol.   M. S.
SEE ALSO: CHOLESTEROL, FATTY ACID.

Lanthanum (LANN-thu-num) Lanthanum is a soft, gray, chemically-reactive metal. Being so rare, it is now of academic interest only.

Lanthanum is the first element of the fifteen element series in the RARE EARTH or lanthanide group. The compounds of most of the other lanthanide elements are colored and have magnetic properties. Lanthanum compounds are colorless and do not have magnetic properties.

Lanthanum and the lanthanide elements are quite vigorously reactive. In moist air they readily combine with the oxygen to form OXIDES. The rare earths are generally found together in compound form in minerals. Most lanthanide elements are difficult to purify.

Lanthanum (symbol La) has atomic number 57. It has an atomic weight of 138.91 (138.92, O=16).   J. R. S.
SEE ALSO: ATOM, ELEMENTS

Laplace, Pierre Simon, Marquis de (1749-1827) Laplace was a French astronomer and mathematician. He developed a theory about the origin of the solar system, and, although it was later proved incorrect, it did help astronomers better understand double stars and spiral nebulae.

The son of a farmer, Laplace was born at Beaumont-en-Auge in Normandy. He attended a military school in Beaumont, where he immediately revealed his mathematical genius. When he was twenty years old, he was appointed professor of mathematics at the military school in Paris. In 1816 he was elected one of the forty Immortals of the French Academy of Science, the highest possible honor to bestow on a Frenchman.   D. H. J.
SEE ALSO: NEBULA; STAR, DOUBLE

Lapwing see Plover

Lard see Fat, Pig

Lark The American horned lark and the European skylark are true larks. The meadowlark is a blackbird. Larks sing during flight. The horned lark has a less tuneful song than the skylark. Several attempts to introduce the skylark into America have failed.

The horned lark, as its name suggests, has tufts of black hornlike feathers on its head. It has a yellow throat with a black collar, and a streaked brown body. There are about 14 subspecies in North America. These birds gather in large flocks, usually walking instead of hopping. They nest on the ground, in depressions filled with grass and feathers.

Their diet consists of insects in the summer and grass and weed seeds in the winter. Horned larks occur throughout America except in the southeast.

The skylark is similar in habits and coloration to the horned lark but lacks horns.
                                    J. C. K.

Skylark

Larkspur see Delphinium

Courtesy Society For Visual Education, Inc.
Worm-like larva of the Io moth

Larva (LAHR-vuh) A larva is a young animal that is not fully developed, but is able to move about and feed itself. It changes into an adult animal that usually looks quite different. This change is called META-MORPHOSIS. The *tadpole* of the FROG, the *caterpillars* of BUTTERFLIES and moths, the *grubs* of BEETLES, and the *maggots* of flies are larvae.

Many larvae live in the ocean. They are part of the tiny animals and plants that float in the water as PLANKTON. The larvae of sponges, jellyfish and other coelenterates, mollusks, and crustaceans move with the drift of the ocean, but have to be produced in large numbers to survive the preying of fish and water mammals.

Larvae that live in the ocean swim about freely by means of *cilia,* hairlike structures that beat in the water. The cilia also help the larva to feed by sweeping currents of water containing food into the mouth. Many larvae have delicate, lobed arms that help them to float and paddle through the water.

The larvae of insects, such as fly maggots, are mostly land-living, although some insects breed in water and produce gill-bearing *naiads*—larvae that live in water. These larvae later metamorphose into insects with wings that fly in air and live on land. This change is often so drastic that an intermediate stage, the pupa, bridges the gap between the immature larva and the mature

Mosquito larvae spend the development time entirely under water

Courtesy Society For Visual Education, Inc.

adult. The tissues of the larva are broken down inside the silken or papery pupa case, and new adult tissues are formed from growth centers called *imaginal disks*. When the pupa breaks open, a new adult insect emerges. This is the way CATERPILLARS change into MOTHS and butterflies.

Much of the history of animal life on earth has been discovered by studying the larval forms of animals. The relationships between animals can be understood more clearly by comparing their young stages. Most animals are rather similar in the earliest stages of development. The ciliated *amphiblastula* (larva of sponges) and the *planula* (larva of coelenterates) resemble the blastula stages of all higher animals.

The flatworms, nemertean worms, annelid worms, and mollusks all have a *trochophore* larva that reveals their common origin. This larva is distinctive in its tuft of cilia at the crown and an equatorial band of cilia. The marine arthropods (CRUSTACEA) have a rather different larva, the *nauplius,* which has three pairs of appendages. However, the resemblance of arthropods to annelids is so striking in many of their characteristics that this indicates that arthropods, too, have primitively shared a trochophore origin.

An entirely different group of animals has developed from the *dipleurula* type of larva. The discovery that echinoderms (starfish, sea urchins) and chordates are related came through study of the larval form. Although sedentary starfish are radially organized as adults, they are bilaterally symmetrical as larvae. This fact ties them to the beginnings of vertebrate animals, as does the fact that primitive chordates such as the acorn worm, *Balanoglossus,* and some tunicates have a dipleurula larva. The dipleurula larva has a longitudinal looped band of cilia and often has arms that propel it through the water.

B. B. G.

SEE ALSO: EMBRYOLOGY, EVOLUTION

Laryngitis (lair-enn-JYE-tuhss) Laryngitis is inflammation of the LARYNX, or voice box. It can be caused by a bad cold (virus infection), irritation by dust, gas, chemicals, or tobacco smoke.

The voice becomes hoarse or is completely lost. Singers and speakers may lose their voices from excessive use.   B. M. H.

Larynx (LAIR-inks) Behind the mouth cavity is the pharynx. It continues into the *voice box* or larynx. The larynx opens into the main air tube (*tracheal*) leading to the lungs. Sound is made when exhaled air vibrates or moves vocal cords in the voice box. Vocal cords are folds in the membrane lining the larynx.

In all VERTEBRATES, slits for gills appear during development. Between the slits, cartilages develop to support them. Gill slits and their cartilages, except in fish and amphibians, are changed into other structures during the course of development. The nine cartilages making up the voice box were once gill slit cartilages.

The largest of the cartilages is the *thyroid* cartilage. It is known as the Adam's apple. Ligaments hold the larynx together. It is covered by the epiglottis during swallowing, preventing food from getting into the RESPIRATORY SYSTEM. Freely movable joints, between the thyroid and the ringlike lower *cricoid* cartilage, allow for rotation and gliding movement.

As the body increases in size the larynx also grows. Laryngeal growth steps up at puberty. The Adam's apple becomes prominent in boys and for a period they are unable to control their vocal cords. As these thicken and lengthen the VOICE deepens.   J. C. K.

Laser The name laser came from the phrase Light Amplification with Stimulation by Emission of Radiation. A laser beam is a bright, single-colored light that is compact and directional. Technically, a laser is a monochromatic, columnated, coherent, intense beam of visible light. Gases, liquids, or solids can sometimes absorb light

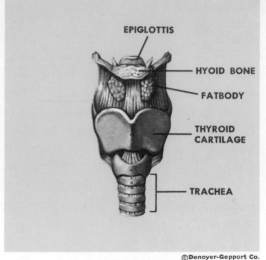

Larynx in man

©Denoyer-Gepport Co.

or electromagnetic radiant energy, store this energy for a while and then, when triggered, emit this energy almost instantly.

Since the development of the first laser in 1960 by Maiman, many of its wonders have been unfolded. It has been used to repair detached retinas within the eye by welding. It can both stimulate and destroy cell tissue. It is used for accurate timing devices, for communication, for metal cutting, and in photography.   M. B. C.

SEE ALSO: ELECTROMAGNETIC RADIATION, MASER.

Latent heat Latent heat is the HEAT absorbed when a substance changes its state without a change in temperature. For example, ice at $0°$ C absorbs heat when it melts to form water at $0°$C.

SEE: HEAT OF REACTION, PHYSICAL STATES AND CHANGES

Lateral Lateral means situated at or proceeding from the side. In botany and zoology, it means attached to one or both sides of the *median* (middle) *plane* of an organ, body or limb. For example, the arm is lateral to the neck.

Latex (LAY-tecks) Latex is a milky liquid produced by certain plants and trees, such as the RUBBER tree, milkweed, and poppy. Unlike SAP, it flows between the layers of the bark. Most rubber is made from latex produced by *Hevea brasiliensis,* the rubber tree.

Lathe A lathe is a machine tool which rotates a piece of wood or metal while the cutting tool moves along or across the work. Cylinders and other rounded pieces are cut on a lathe.

SEE: MACHINERY

Latitude Latitude is the distance of any place from the EQUATOR measured directly north and south. It is expressed in degrees. Each degree represents about 70 miles. There are 360 degrees around the earth.

SEE: EARTH, LONGITUDE

Laudanum see Opium

Laurel True laurel plants are evergreen trees and SHRUBS. The trees may grow as high as fifty feet while the shrubs may grow to be fifteen feet tall. The laurel is often grown as a large potted plant. It is easily pruned to grow in interesting shapes. These plants are often used on terraces as ornaments. Laurels have small yellow flowers and dark purple berries. Florists often use the dark green glossy leaves in flower arrangements. Oils and some medicines are extracted from laurel berries and leaves

Laurel plants are grown from seeds or cuttings. They should be planted in rich, humus-filled soil and kept moist. They must be protected from winter cold. Laurels do not make good house plants because of the dry heat.

Laurel plant

The ancient Greeks used crowns of laurel leaves to honor winners of the Pythian games. Later, laurel crowns indicated academic achievement.

SASSAFRAS, CINNAMON, and AVOCADO trees belong to the laurel family. The plant popularly known as *mountain laurel* is not a laurel. It belongs to the same group of plants as HEATHER. M. R. L.

Lava (LAH-vuh) Lava is hot, melted (molten) rock that is forced to the surface of the earth. It may flow rapidly from an active VOLCANO, or it may move out slowly from cracks in the earth's surface. Millions of years ago there were many volcanoes and lava flows.

When hot molten rock is found under the surface, it is termed *magma*. If magma cools and hardens under the surface it forms intrusive (*plutonic*) igneous rock.

Lava on the surface cools much faster than magma found deep within the earth. As the result of faster cooling, lava will have a fine-grained crystalline structure while magma will be coarse-grained. Sometimes lava is blown into the air and cools rapidly.

Rocks formed from lava are called *extrusive* igneous rocks. *Obsidian* is a lava that has cooled so rapidly that it has not crystallized but has become a glassy substance called "volcanic glass."

When lava that is filled with vapor or gas hardens rapidly, many tiny pores remain in the rock after the disengagement of the vapors. This rock is a kind of frothy obsidian that will float on water and is called *pumice*

The major types of igneous rocks that are formed from lava are *basalt,* a fine-grained black rock, and *granite,* a coarser grained rock in a variety of colors. These igneous rocks formed from lava make up much of the bedrock of the earth's crust. H. S. G.

SEE ALSO: INTRUSION, MAGMA, ROCKS

Dried and cracked lava rock
Courtesy Society For Visual Education, Inc.

Lavender

Antoine Lavoisier

Lavender Lavender is any of several sweet-smelling European plants of the MINT family. Its pale purple flowers give the name "lavender" to this shade of purple. Oil of lavender, distilled from the flowers, is used in PERFUME and soap. Dried leaves keep their odor for a long time, and are used to scent linens and clothes.

Lavoisier, Antoine Laurent (lah-VWAH-zyeh, AHN-twahn loh-RAHN) (1743-1794) Lavoisier was the "father of modern CHEMISTRY." A brilliant research chemist, he was the first person to explain fire scientifically. He discovered, through careful research, that burning was the result of the mixing of oxygen with the material being burned. It was Lavoisier who developed the modern concept of the element. He and PIERRE SIMON LAPLACE carried out the first *thermo-electrical* (thermo coming from the Greek word meaning "heat") investigations and developed an apparatus to measure linear (pertaining to lines) and cubical (pertaining to cubes) expansions.

This great chemist was born of aristocratic parents in Paris. His father gave him an excellent education in the fields of mathematics, astronomy, chemistry, and botany. In 1766 he was awarded a gold medal by the French Academy of Sciences for a plan of lighting the city streets. Two years later he was invited to become a member of the Academy and proceeded to pass through all the grades in the Academy, becoming its director at the age of forty-two and treasurer at the age of forty-eight.

When Lavoisier became the government farmer general of revenues, he set up a model farm to show the advantages of scientific agriculture. He loaned money to two French towns without interest to buy barley during the famine of 1788. Always vitally interested in civic and economic problems, he was asked at various times to investigate taxation, public education, coinage, social conditions. In 1789 he even drew up instructions for the deputies to the states-general to which he was elected as an alternate deputy. It was his work that led to the establishment of the METRIC SYSTEM in France.

Born an aristocrat, Lavoisier was condemned to the guillotine by a revolutionary tribunal. When he was found guilty on the morning of May 8, 1794, beheaded that afternoon, and dumped into a common grave, Joseph Lagrange, the prominent mathematician and Lavoisier's colleague, said, "It required only a moment to sever his head, and perhaps a century will not be sufficient to produce another like it."

D. H. J.

Lawrencium (luh-RENN-see-um) Lawrencium is the very newest chemical element. It was discovered in April, 1961, by scientists (Albert Ghiorso, Torbjorn Sikkeland, Almon Larsh and Robert Latimer) of the University of California Radiation Laboratory. It is the 103rd element. Lawrencium is so unstable that its half-life is estimated at only eight seconds. It was named after Ernest Lawrence, founder of the laboratory in which it was first detected.

Lawrencium was produced by bombarding CALIFORNIUM with BORON nuclei, accelerated in a cyclotron. It is of only theoretical interest at present and the supply is very, very small. The mass number of its most stable isotope is 257.　　　　　　　　　　　D. L. D.

SEE ALSO: ATOM, ELEMENTS

Lead Lead is a soft but heavy METAL. It has been known for a long time. Roman ruins contain many examples of lead used for water pipes. It was called *plumbum*. The English word *plumber* was derived from it. The symbol of lead is Pb.

Pure lead is bright and silvery but will tarnish in air. Aside from this tarnishing, lead will resist further CORROSION much better than most metals. The DENSITY of lead is 11.3 grams per cubic centimeter, and its melting point is 327.4°C. Its atomic number is 82 and its atomic weight is 207.19 (207.21, O=16). It has several isotopes, mainly 206, 207, and 208.

The most important lead ore is lead sulfide or GALENA. It is found in veins and usually with other metals. Flotation is used to concentrate the ore. Then by roasting, most of the sulfide is converted to lead oxide.

$$2PbS + 3O_2 \longrightarrow 2PbO + 2SO_2$$

After improving the quality of the ore, coke and fresh sulfide are added. Limestone is also added to act as a flux. As with iron, lead smelting is done in a blast furnace:

$$PbS + 2PbO \longrightarrow 3Pb + SO_2$$
$$2PbO + C \longrightarrow 2Pb + CO_2$$

The product is metallic lead with by-product gases of sulfur dioxide and carbon dioxide. The metal so obtained is not pure enough for most commercial use. Sometimes the Parkes process of removing silver is used to purify the lead, but purification is usually done by the electrolytic method. The solution used as an electrolyte is lead fluorosilicate, $PbSiF_6$, and a little fluorosilicic acid, H_2SiF_6. Pure lead migrates in the form of Pb^{+2} ions from the positive to the negative pole.

Important compounds of lead include lead monoxide, PbO or yellow litharge, and red lead, Pb_3O_4, used in storage batteries. White lead, $Pb (OH)_2 \cdot 2PbCO_3$, is used in paints. Ethyl gasolines to reduce the "knocking" of automobile and airplane engines contain tetraethyl lead, $Pb(C_2H_5)_4$.

The widespread use of lead compounds in industry and the home makes it important that everyone be aware of lead poisoning, or *plumbism*. Acute poisoning from lead is very rare.　　　　E. Y. K.

SEE ALSO: ELECTROLYSIS, METALS

Leaflet A leaflet is one of two or more separate small blades into which a compound leaf is divided. Leaflets are either in rows on the sides of the stem or spread out from its tip.

SEE: LEAVES

Leather Leather is often used for shoes, luggage, coats, belts, purses, and gloves. It is made from animal skins that have been chemically treated to soften and preserve them.

Skins from many animals can be made into leather. Ostrich, goat, lamb, cattle, horse, and reptile skins are some of those used.

Leather has been made for thousands of years by curing skins in tannic acid. Tannic acid is made from tree parts such as bark, roots, and leaves. A good tannin came from the bark of the American chestnut tree. When a blight killed almost all of them, tannins had to be imported. The *quebracho* tree in South America is one important source. Tannic acid acts on the gelatin compounds in skin, changing them into the compounds found in leather. Hair is removed by lime solutions and dehairing machines.

At the present time, tannin is less important in the leather industry. Synthetic tannins and chromium salts are used.　　　J. C. K.

SEE ALSO: COW, SKIN, SKIN MODIFICATIONS

Leather hanging during the tanning process

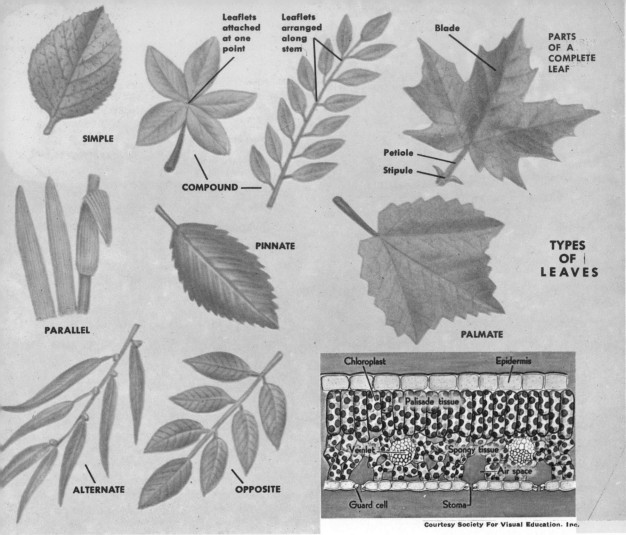

Leaflets attached at one point

Leaflets arranged along stem

SIMPLE

COMPOUND —

Blade

PARTS OF A COMPLETE LEAF

Petiole

Stipule

PINNATE

TYPES OF LEAVES

PARALLEL

PALMATE

ALTERNATE

OPPOSITE

Chloroplast   Epidermis

Palisade tissue

Veinlet   Spongy tissue

Air space

Guard cell   Stoma

Cross-section of a leaf

Leaves Roots, stems, and leaves are the main parts that carry on most of the life processes for higher plants. Each has a job to do. Leaves make food (PHOTOSYNTHESIS) for the other parts. They also permit air to enter tiny openings. Some leaves do other tasks. There are storage leaves on celery and rhubarb. Spines of gooseberry bushes and cactus are types of leaves. Some leaves can trap insects as in the pitcher plant. Other leaves make a new plant (PROPAGATION).

A typical leaf has certain basic parts. The blade or *lamina* is attached to a stalk or *petiole*. This stalk twists and turns the blade toward the sun. At the base of a petiole is a bud. The blade of a *simple* leaf is in one piece, as in elm.

A *compound* leaf has several leaves or *leaflets* on the main petiole, as in locust. Only one bud is at the petiole base of the compound leaf.

Size of leaves varies from very tiny to over 30 feet long. They usually have two leafy structures at their base called *stipules* which protect the young leaf bud. In some plants stipules may be missing or modified into thorns or tendrils. A leaf which lacks petioles is termed *sessile*. Veins form the skeleton of the leaf. In MONOCOTYLEDONS they run parallel to each other. In DICOTYLEDONS the veins form a network. If there is one main rib with veins branching out from it, the leaf has *pinnate venation*. If there are several main veins originating from the petiole with many side branches, the leaf has *palmate venation*.

The margin or edge of leaves is used in classification. They may be *smooth* or *entire*, *serrated* or saw-toothed, or *lobed*; some leaves are variations of these. Leaves are arranged on stems in one of three patterns. One leaf

948

per node is called *alternate*. Two leaves may be *opposite* to each other. When three or more leaves circle a node it is a *whorled* arrangement.

INTERNAL STRUCTURE

The top layer of cells or epidermis serves as a protection. Some plants have an extra layer of *cutin* covering these cells. Just under the epidermis are column-like cells, *palisade parenchyma,* containing large numbers of chloroplasts. Much of the food-making occurs here. The next layers of cells, *spongy parenchyma,* are loosely packed with numerous air spaces. Veins or VASCULAR BUNDLES are scattered throughout the leaf. They contain xylem and phloem cells. This permits a continuous set of tubes and vessels for conduction of materials up and down the leaf, stem and root. The bottom of the leaf is the lower epidermis. This is the surface where most of the holes or *stomata* are found. Each opening is surrounded by two guard cells. They open and close at various times of the day depending upon environmental conditions. When open the air comes in and water gets out. A single tree may lose 100 gallons of water per day. TRANSPIRATION is the loss of water vapor. *Guttation* is the oozing out or loss of liquid from water-secreting glands in some leaves.

Leaves are temporary structures. At some point they may fall off and new leaves may or may not develop, depending upon the life of a plant. In the temperate zone, the change from warm to cold weather causes leaves to drop. They are DECIDUOUS. Some leaves stay on until new leaves are produced. They are EVERGREEN. Some have stayed on for two to ten years. Cold weather causes a band of parenchyma cells (abscission layer) at the base of the petiole to become soft and gelatinous. A corky row of cells also forms. As these cells begin to separate, only the vascular bundles are holding a leaf to the branch. These soon give way and the leaf falls.

Zerophytes are plants in dry regions. Stomata are in depressed pockets to prevent water loss. On *mesophytes,* they are even with the epidermis. These live in temperate regions. Wet climates produce *hydrophytes* with raised stomata. Water lilies have them on top of giant floating leaves. H. J. C.

SEE ALSO: BUDS; PHOTOSYNTHESIS; PLANT; PLANT TISSUE; PLANTS, CLASSIFICATION OF; TREE

✳ THINGS TO DO

MAKING YOUR OWN LEAF GUIDE

A leaf guide will be very useful when you go on hikes through the summer season or when you go away to camp. Trees are easily identified by the kind of leaf they bear. Here are several techniques to use in preparing the guidebook.

1 Collect fresh leaves. Be sure to pick the entire leaf if it is compound in structure. Lay the leaves flat between many layers of newspapers. Place a weight (pile of books) on top of the stack. On the second day replace the newspapers with dry ones. Most leaves will be dried and pressed in three days. These may be mounted on paper with glue. Then shellac the whole surface.

2 For spatter prints place the leaf on a sheet of paper. Hold a piece of fine mesh screening over the leaf. Push a toothbrush, dipped in tempera paint, back and forth over the screen. Be careful that drops do not form on the underside.

3 Leaves may be dipped into hot wax for preservation Hang the leaf up by the petiole until the parafin sets.

4 Place a leaf on blueprint paper. Expose it to the sun for a minute or two. Remove the leaf and immediately dip the paper into a pan of water. Then put it between two paper towels to dry.

5 Grease the outside of a glass jar. Hold this area over a candle flame until it becomes dark gray. Place a leaf, underside up, on a stack of papers which will act as a cushion. Roll the smokey area of the jar over the leaf. Then put a white sheet of paper over the leaf. Roll again with a clean jar. The details of the leaf will appear on the paper. These are called smoke prints.

Buchsbaum

Common leech, also called bloodsucker, showing suckers

Leech Some of these animals are ECTOPARASITES. They suck blood from other animals. Others feed upon worms, snails, and insect larvae. They are related to EARTHWORMS, and are like them in many ways. Their bodies always have 33 sections or segments, plus many creases or *annuli*.

Leeches have suckers at the ends of their bodies. The anterior smaller one may be behind or around the mouth. Both suckers are used for anchorage in locomotion and, if parasitic, for attachment to the HOST. Leeches are classified on the basis of whether they have chitinous teeth in a muscular pumping pharynx, or no teeth but a muscular proboscis that can be extended. The pharynx opens into a stomach with 11 pairs of lateral pouches. The rest of the digestive tract and the excretory system are typical of ANNELIDA.

Nervous systems show more fusion and specialization than those of other annelids. The well developed COELOM in this phylum, has been invaded by CONNECTIVE TISSUE and is only a series of tissue spaces.   J. C. K.

Leek The leek is a hardy garden vegetable with a mild onion flavor. A relative of onion, garlic, and chives, the leek flower stem grows to about two feet. The flower appears in large, compact balls. It looks something like an onion except that it does not grow a large bulb but has a thickened stem.

Leek

Leeuwenhoek, Anton van (LAY-vuhn-hohk) (1632-1723) Leeuwenhoek was a Dutch scientist who discovered BACTERIA, or "little beasties" as he called them. Interested in making microscopes and then studying everything he could find, Leeuwenhoek happened to observe a drop of rain water taken from a barrel beside his house. He discovered that it was filled with "wretched beasties moving about very nimbly." He wrote extensively and drew pictures of what he saw, and although he did not realize that the bacteria he was studying caused disease, his work soon enabled scientists (SPALLANZANI and PASTEUR) to make that discovery.

An uneducated man who never learned Latin, then the language of scholars, Leeuwenhoek lived his entire life in Delft, Holland. As a boy he was trained to clerk in a dry goods store, and part of his job was to examine cloth beneath a magnifying glass, but whenever possible he would examine other things beneath his glass. He later owned his own dry goods shop, but in his spare time he pursued his great interest in close examination of the things about him. He learned to grind lenses and build microscopes of his own. Some of the 247 instruments he built magnified the size of an object as much as 270 times.

When Leeuwenhoek was about forty years old and a widower with a grown family, he decided to spend the remainder of his life doing what he wanted. He sold his shop and devoted all of his time to making observations through his microscopes and building better and more powerful microscopes. He studied bacteria, yeast cells, and blood corpuscles. He also drew pictures of muscle fibers and described how the blood circulated in the body.

When he passed away at the age of ninety-two, Leeuwenhoek was famous, yet possibly his greatest contribution to science was that he had prepared the way for Louis Pasteur to open the whole new field of BACTERIOLOGY.   D. H. J.

Leghorn see Chicken

Like that of all legumes, the seed pod of the bean splits along both sides

Lemming

Legume Plants which have a true pod or legume are grouped into one large family. They may be herbs, shrubs, trees, or climbing plants. They are rich in protein, vitamin B, and minerals. Next to the grass family, legumes are the most important plants to man. They are used for food, drugs, forage, and pleasure. A few are poisonous. Beans, locust, clover, vetch, sweet pea, and wisteria are all examples of legumes.

Legumes may be annuals, biennials, or perennials. Leaves are alternately arranged on the stem. Most plants possess compound leaves but a few have simple ones. FLOWERS are usually perfect and often butterfly-shaped. Most common inflorescences are racemes, heads, or spikes. Individual flowers have 5 petals and sepals, often 10 stamens and a single carpel in the pistil. One petal forms the banner or standard at the top. Two petals form lateral projections and the last two make the keel at the bottom.

Dry, dehiscent pods split longitudinally along both sides or seams called sutures. Some legumes, such as vetch, explode their seeds great distances. The pod of alfalfa is greatly coiled. Peanut fruit does not dehisce at all. It develops below ground level.

Nitrogen-fixing bacteria live symbiotically with legumes in nodules or growths on their roots. They are the agents for transforming free gas into compounds usable by plants.

Legumes belong to the family Leguminosae. There are 500 genera and 14,000 species in this group.　　　H. J. C.
SEE ALSO: ANGIOSPERMS; ECONOMIC BOTANY; PLANTS, CLASSIFICATION OF

Lemming A lemming is a small, thickset rodent which looks like a large, short-tailed meadow mouse. There are several kinds of lemmings, but the one most written about is the lemming of Scandinavia. Closely related species are found in Siberia and the Arctic.

These animals are like miniature, short-eared, yellowish rabbits. They have large heads and short, thick legs. They eat vegetable food and build nests of bark or grass in some sheltered nook. They raise two broods of four to six young every year. They do not hibernate but force their way under the snow, searching for food.

The migration of the Scandinavian lemmings is one of the marvels of rodent life. Every few years they become so numerous that the mountains cannot support them. At irregular intervals, great swarms of lemmings start for new territory and do not stop for rivers, lakes, or mountains. Eating everything they can find on the way, they fall prey to disease, larger animals, and birds. These armies of rodents have gnawed through haystacks and crossed marshes. When they come to the ocean, they boldly swim out, in their ignorance of its size, and are drowned. Their population problem is solved for a few more years.　　　J. K. K.
SEE ALSO: RODENTIA

Lemon see Citrus fruit

Lemur

Lemur (LEE-mer) Lemur is the name given to a group of animals which are related to monkeys. Lemurs are generally smaller than monkeys, and their bodies are covered with fur. Lemurs belong to the order PRIMATES which includes monkeys, apes, and man. Lemurs are some of the most primitive animals of the primate order. Most of them can be found on the island of Madagascar. Some live in Asia and Africa. Lemurs usually live in trees although some are known to dwell among rocks. Their diet includes fruit, leaves, buds, shoots, birds, birds' eggs, insects, reptiles, and seeds.

Most lemurs have long faces very similar to foxes'. Their eyes are large and deep set. Most of them are nocturnal. Perhaps their strange appearance and their habit of stirring quietly at night accounts for the name *lemur,* which means "ghost." There are a few that are active during the day. Lemurs' eyes are directed in such a way that they are unable to focus both eyes at the same time. Their vision is not binocular.

Lemurs have tails of varying lengths which are not as useful to them as are the tails of monkeys. Lemurs vary in size, in color, and in general appearance. The *indri* is the largest of the lemurs. This lemur can walk on its hind legs. It does not have a long tail. The *ruffed lemur* is also among the larger of the group. The *mouse lemur* is very small. When full grown it is about the size of a small rat. It has a very long tail. During certain periods when food is scarce, this lemur sleeps, living off the food which has been stored up in its long tail.   G. A. D.
SEE ALSO: MONKEY

Lens, animal see Eye

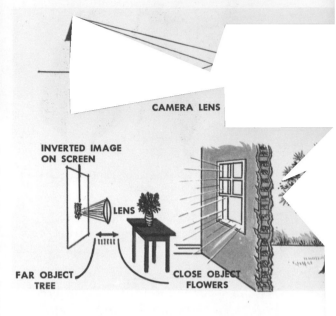

CAMERA LENS

INVERTED IMAGE ON SCREEN

LENS

FAR OBJECT TREE

CLOSE OBJECT FLOWERS

Lens, man-made An object seen through a lens looks bigger or smaller. A lens has a curved surface. If the surface is curved outward, it will make things look bigger. If curved inward, it will make them look smaller. A curved surface bends the light rays passing through the lens. The amount of bending depends on the curve of the surface and speed of light in the lens. Light travels more slowly in solid materials than in air.

Lenses are now made of glass or plastics. Precious gems were used at first for lack of other clear material.

Optical instruments use lenses to magnify an image or to make it appear smaller. MICROSCOPE lenses magnify tiny objects at very close distances. TELESCOPES or BINOCULARS magnify objects at very great distances.

CAMERA lenses focus the light from objects to form a small image on a film. The film image may be projected or enlarged to any desired size through the use of lens systems.

The lenses in eyeglasses correct the vision of people whose eyes (which have "living" lenses) cannot focus light on the retina. *Contact lenses* correct certain vision defects. They are plastic lenses which float on the

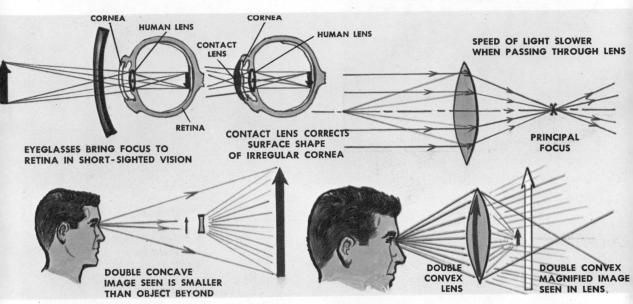

CORNEA — HUMAN LENS — CORNEA — HUMAN LENS — CONTACT LENS — RETINA — SPEED OF LIGHT SLOWER WHEN PASSING THROUGH LENS — PRINCIPAL FOCUS

EYEGLASSES BRING FOCUS TO RETINA IN SHORT-SIGHTED VISION

CONTACT LENS CORRECTS SURFACE SHAPE OF IRREGULAR CORNEA

DOUBLE CONCAVE IMAGE SEEN IS SMALLER THAN OBJECT BEYOND

DOUBLE CONVEX LENS — DOUBLE CONVEX MAGNIFIED IMAGE SEEN IN LENS

There are two basic shapes to man-made lenses. The variations of these are used in many ways

tear layer over the cornea. Some optical corrections which formerly required very thick eyeglasses to make light rays meet properly now are corrected by nearly invisible, tiny contact lenses.

The *convex* lens (also called *converging* or *positive* lens) is one of the major kinds. It is thicker at the center than at the edges (bulging outward). Light rays traveling parallel to the lens' axis bend (or converge) after passing through the lens and meet at a point beyond the lens called the *principal focus*. (F). The distance from the center of the lens to this point is called the *focal length*. All lenses have such a focus on each side of the lens.

When viewing an object through a convex lens, images of different size may be formed, depending upon how far the object is from the lens.

The convex lens may be compared to a pinhole in a card to show the changes of image size with changing distances. The effect of light passing through a point is the same for the pinhole and the lens, but a great deal more light passes through the lens. The convex lens may also be compared to a set of prisms which bring rays to a point.

It is possible to bring objects at different distances into focus on a paper screen. Very slight changes in the distance of the lens to the screen will sharpen the focus in a picture of, for example, either the view outside a window, or the frame of the window itself,

or an object inside the room between the lens and the window.

The image of a light bulb filament or candle flame can be formed on a screen by holding a convex lens at a proper distance from it. Focal distance varies with lens shape.

Concave lenses (the other major type) spread light apart. They are thicker at the edges than at the center (bridge inward). The image seen through a concave lens is right-side-up and smaller than the object. The only place the viewer sees this type of image, called a *virtual image,* is by looking into the lens itself—not on a screen.

Another example of virtual image is in a convex lens used as a magnifier when it is held closer to an object than its focal length. The virtual image thus seen also is right-side-up, but enlarged. Virtual images cannot be projected on a screen.

Portions of lenses act as prisms do in separating light into the SPECTRUM. This causes violet light to be focused closer to the convex lens than red. Hazy colors appear at the edge of images created by cheaply-ground *chromatic* lenses. *Achromatic* lenses have this defect corrected either by changing the curved surface of the lens or by combining lenses of glass with different light-refracting properties.   E. I. D.

SEE ALSO: EYE, MAGNIFYING POWER, OPTICAL INSTRUMENTS, OPTOMETRY, PRISM, PROJECTOR, REFRACTION

Lentil plant

Lentil Lentil is an ANNUAL plant of the pea family. The pods, which hold two lens-shaped seeds also called "lentils," are ground into meal when dry and used in soups.
SEE: LEGUME

Leo Leo, or the Lion, is a group of stars that seem to outline the shape of a lion in the sky. Leo can be seen in the night sky in the summer time. It is one of the signs of the ZODIAC.

The stars at one end of this CONSTELLATION form a pattern like a sickle. The sickle is the front of the lion. There is a triangle of stars at the other end that marks the hind quarters of the lion.

This constellation was called a lion because the sun was in Leo in the summer time. Lions are associated with the tropical regions and hot climates. Lions are supposed to be very powerful. In the summer time the sun seems hottest and most powerful. It was imagined that Leo had some effect on the heat and power of the sun. Another legend, from Greek mythology, tells that Leo was once a ferocious lion that stalked in the forest of Nemea. No hunter would dare to go after him. Hercules finally went and killed the lion. Jupiter placed the lion in the sky.   C. L. K.

Leo, the Lion

Leonardo da Vinci

Leonardo da Vinci (VIN-chee) (1452-1519) Leonardo da Vinci is best known as an artist, but he was interested in almost everything. The period in which he lived is called the *Renaissance,* meaning *rebirth,* because people were rediscovering the learning of ancient Greece and Rome after many centuries in which free inquiry was discouraged. The Renaissance people were going on to create new kinds of art and to make scientific discoveries. Leonardo represents this period perhaps better than anyone else because he explored so many subjects.

He investigated such scientific areas as anatomy, astronomy, botany, geology, and engineering. In the field of art, he worked with painting, sculpture, and architecture. His notebooks were filled with ideas and sketches of inventions, including designs for an airplane which showed that he understood the principles of flight long before they were demonstrated.

Born in Vinci, near Florence, Italy, Leonardo was the son of a village notary. As a boy he showed remarkable skill in solving difficult problems in mathematics and engineering. He also showed great talent in painting; thus he was apprenticed to An-

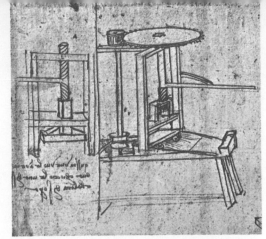

Many of da Vinci's inventions, such as the double crane and printing press, anticipated devices that would be perfected centuries later

drea del Verrocchio from whom he received training as a painter, sculptor and goldsmith. Although Leonardo completed only a few paintings, he soon surpassed Verrocchio, and when he was in his early thirties, Leonardo left the studio of his teacher and went to Milan, where he entered the service of the Duke of Milan. There he painted *The Last Supper*, one of the finest paintings in the history of art. In addition, he completed a full-sized, clay model of the gigantic horse for Francesco Sforza's tomb.

Not long after Leonardo joined the Duke, the city of Milan was occupied by the French, under the direction of King Louis XII. The Duke was forced to flee. The huge clay statue of the horse was destroyed, and nothing remains of it today. Leonardo returned to Florence and soon afterward painted the famous portrait of Madame Gioconda—known as *The Mona Lisa*. It is considered by many art critics to be his masterpiece. The lady's smile has been the object of much speculation.

Between July, 1502, and March, 1503, Leonardo served Cesare Borgia as architect and engineer in his military campaign in central Italy. When he returned to Florence, he began two of the greatest projects of his life, one scientific and the other artistic. He worked out a plan by which the Arno River could be diverted to make a navigable waterway to the city of Florence. The second project was the painting of a battle scene to decorate the great hall of the Palazzo Vecchio. Both projects ended in failure.

At the age of 54, Leonardo returned to Milan to serve the French king. Six years later he went to Rome to help reconstruct and decorate St. Peter's Cathedral. Leonardo was then persuaded to go to France, where he lived in splendor until he died.

A man of wide interests, Leonardo studied the formation of rocks, the effects of waterfalls, the effects of the weather, and the movements of the stars and planets. He invented weapons of war, such as the tank and the machine gun; he drew military maps for war campaigns; he designed a canal system for the city of Milan, part of which is still in use; he invented the first elevator; and he made life-sized mechanical toys to charm his patrons.

Leonardo's remarkable knowledge of anatomy and psychology are revealed in his paintings and sculptures. D. H. J.

Leopard see Cat family

Leprosy (LEPP-ruh-see) Leprosy is a chronic, infectious disease affecting the skin and producing certain changes in the nerves. While said to be passed from one person to another, the danger is relatively slight. The disease first came to man's notice because of the victims's coarse, thickened skin and some deformities.

The immediate cause is a rod-shaped germ called *Bacillus leprae,* discovered by Hansen in 1874. Hence, the disease is called *Hansen's disease.* There are two types of leprosy found in the southern part of the United States. In one type, nodules, which later break down into ulcers, form on the skin. In the other, the nerves of the extremities become thickened and painful. The ancients called leprosy an "unclean" disease. This is not necessarily so, but certainly scrupulous cleanliness and sanitation are necessary. The common housefly has been blamed for carrying the disease, but this is not yet proven. H. K. S.

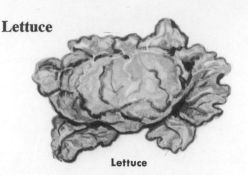
Lettuce

Lettuce It is a hardy herb that lives for only one growing season. Many large leaves grow in circles on the short stem. Flowers are tongue-shaped and grow in clusters. The fruit of this vegetable is dry.

There are commonly three kinds of lettuce grown. Head lettuce is round like cabbage. Romaine lettuce forms long heads with the inside leaves bleached out. The third variety is loose leaf lettuce. This VEGETABLE has low caloric value but does have vitamins and minerals.

The FLOWER stalk develops an inflorescence or panicle. The FRUIT or achene has parachute-like tufts of hair useful in seed dispersal. Lettuce belongs to the Compositae family. H. J. C.

Leukemia (loo-KEEM-ee-uh) Leukemia is a disease affecting the white BLOOD cells. The white blood cells, or corpuscles, normally increase in number when there is infection in the body. In leukemia they increase to enormous numbers without an infection in the body. The cause of leukemia is unknown, although there is a possibility that an obscure VIRUS is involved.

In leukemia there is an uncontrolled production of white blood cells. Some of these are produced in the bone marrow, lymph nodes, and SPLEEN. These white corpuscles are immature, abnormal, and not capable of fighting infection as are normal white blood cells. Therefore, a person with leukemia may have an abundance of white blood cells, yet die of infection. Death is often caused by bleeding into vital organs, such as the brain, or by infections causing PNEUMONIA. Leukemia may have a rapid course (acute) or last for many years (chronic). Persons exposed to the atomic bomb blasts over Hiroshima and Nagasaki in World War II have shown a high incidence of leukemia. In healthy persons, the white blood cells number approximately 5,000 to 12,000 per cubic millimeter of blood. In leukemia they may increase to several hundred thousand. Examination of a blood smear under the microscope will often show the presence of leukemia. It might be necessary to put a needle into the sternum and aspirate the marrow. This will almost always prove or disprove the diagnosis.

B. M. H.

SEE ALSO: CANCER

Levee (LEH-vee) Levees are wide walls formed along river banks to help keep the water in the river bed and prevent flooding. In the spring time or after heavy rains, many rivers overflow into the low lying lands around them. When they overflow they still carry dirt and sediment with them. The flooded water cannot move as fast as it did in the river; therefore, it begins to drop the dirt along the river bank. Eventually the dirt and debris accumulate and form *natural* levees.

These natural levees help to protect the people who live along the river from floods, as the water must reach a higher level to go over the levee. In many places, especially along the Mississippi River, these natural levees are not enough to protect the people, and wide walls or *man-made* levees are built along the river to keep it from flooding. They are made of sandbags and banked earth. J. D. B.

SEE ALSO: DAMS, FLOOD

Lever see Machines, simple

Libra (LYE-bruh) Libra is a group of stars that to ancient people resembled weighing scales. It is visible in the summer time. Libra is not a very

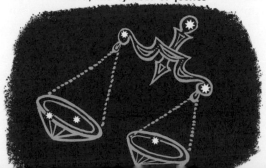
Libra, the symbol of justice

Buchsbaum

Reindeer moss, a lichen

large CONSTELLATION. Its four main stars form a figure like a kite. It is near the bright constellation SCORPIUS. Libra is one of the signs of the ZODIAC.

The sun is in the sign of Libra in the autumn when the days and nights are of equal length. The Romans believed that Libra was the scale of Aestraea, the goddess of justice. She used the scale to weigh the fate of men. One legend is that Libra was a memorial to Mochis, who was said to have invented weights and measures.   C. L. K.

Lichen (LYE-kenn) Lichens are plants that have no flowers, roots, leaves, or stems. They are strange and interesting formations that grow on rocks and along beaches. They live on the bark of trees on the highest mountains. They will completely cover the branches of jungle trees. Some lichens grow farther north than any other plant, as far as the frozen arctic land.

Lichens are a combination of two kinds of plants that aid each other in a kind of partnership (*symbiosis*). One plant is a green or blue-green ALGA which contains CHLOROPHYLL to make food. Algae need moisture to grow, which is supplied by the other partner, *fungus*. FUNGUS, which has no green coloring matter, absorbs and stores water and mineral salts for both plants. Together they are the plants called *lichens*.

Lichens, a class of plants in subkingdom *Thallophyta,* have a plant body called a *thallus*. They are usually placed into three groups: those that resemble a low leaf-like structure, those that grow into an upright shrub form, and those that develop into a flat, crusty plant. In all cases, the fungus must join a specific alga to survive.

Lichens dissolve slowly, producing an acid which disintegrates the rocks to which they cling, and which improves the soil. Such plants that grow on rocks are called *lithophytes*. Lichens decay and mix with the soil, making it richer so that other plants are able to grow in it.

Some lichens that contain STARCH are used for food. Icelanders make bread from lichen called *Iceland moss. Reindeer moss,* another lichen, is eaten by reindeer, caribou, and musk ox. The *manna* eaten by Israelites on the desert, recorded in the Old Testament, was probably a lichen which is still used as food today. Lichens produce colored pigments used in dyeing. A lichen is used in making litmus paper.   P. G. B.

Licorice Licorice is an ANNUAL European plant of the pea family that produces a sweet, brittle, blackish substance also called "licorice." It is used in brewing, in candy-making, and for flavoring. Licorice medicines are used for coughs and as a laxative.
SEE: ANISE

Licorice

Lie detector A lie detector is a device used by modern police forces to help determine if a person is telling the truth. The changes in a person's blood pressure, breathing, pulse, electrical skin resistance, and other activities are measured on a graph. A trained operator is usually able to determine if the questions are answered correctly. A lie detector is also called a *polygraph.*

Life, characteristics of

Life, characteristics of Life, or the condition of being alive, is one of the mysteries of science. All living beings are made of the same materials as nonliving things, but living things can do things that nonliving things cannot do. They can move, grow, and reproduce. They are made of cells. They react to things around them. One can tell living things from non-living things by their characteristics, but it is almost impossible to explain what life is. One can only list the things it does. In other words, one can tell *how* a cat or a rose bush is different from a rock, but cannot tell *why*.

All living things carry on all of the following processes, called characteristics of life. Nonliving things may appear to do some of these, but only living beings can carry on all of these processes.

The first characteristic of life is the *ability to move*. A person can get up and move when he wants to. Plants also move, but the movement can frequently be seen only with a microscope. However, a rock or a piece of paper cannot move unless some force, such as the wind, or a person, makes it move.

The *ability to respond to a stimulus* is an important function of living things. The sun acts as a stimulus for many plants, and they respond to it by moving or turning towards it. If the telephone rings, a person responds to this stimulus by jumping up and running to answer it.

All living things are made of CELLS and *grow* from the inside out. Nonliving things increase their size by adding to the outside. Living things take in food, break it down so they can use it, use part of it for energy and growth, and eliminate parts of it that they cannot use.

Producing offspring, or *reproduction,* is the final characteristic of life. All living things can produce new living beings that are like the parents that produced them. Cats can reproduce more cats, and roses can reproduce more roses.   J. D. B.

SEE ALSO: ANIMAL, PLANT

Life cycle see Aging, Birth, Death

Lift see Aerodynamics

Ligament see Fibrous tissue

Ligature A ligature is a thread of metal or other material, such as catgut, silk, or nylon. They are used to tie off blood vessels during surgical operations. Absorbable sutures will dissolve after several weeks.

Light Light is what the eyes sense and the brain records as sight. Light from an object must reach the eye to be seen. For example, this page can be seen because the sun's light or light from another source is reflected from it into the eyes. If a book is taken into a dark closet, it could not be seen. Most objects are visible because they reflect light from a *luminescent* or glowing source.

The sun is the main source of "natural" light. Other STARS also give off similar light but are extremely distant from Earth. Far less of their light reaches Earth. Light from the sun reaches the earth in about eight minutes. From other stars it takes many years.

Materials which are heated to above 1400° Fahrenheit (800° Centigrade) produce light. Solids and liquids are then *incandescent* (glowing with heat). The particles in a flame, a "red hot" iron rod, or a light bulb filament are sources of light and heat due to the atomic activity of the material. Color and brightness of such materials vary as temperatures go higher or lower. Things which are visibly hot will first glow a dull red, and as the range of temperature goes up, the material approaches "white hot."

Some objects are luminescent without it being necessary for them to be at high temperatures. Certain chemicals when mixed together give off light called *chemiluminescence.* A firefly's tail produces a "cool" light as do some other living organisms. Luminous watch dials, RADIUM substances, and phosphorescent materials glow regardless of the surrounding temperature.

A gas through which an electric current passes will emit light that is not incandescent. The brightness and color of light will not vary from gaseous materials, but depend upon the nature of the gas. Some solid

✳ THINGS TO DO

HOW DO OTHERS SEE YOU?

1 Take two mirrors and set them at right angles to each other.
2 The image of the left side of one's face is caught by the left-hand mirror, reflected in the right-hand mirror and to the eye. The same applies to the image on the right side.
3 Try holding a printed page up to these mirrors as proof that they do show objects the right way.

materials also give off light when an electric current passes through them. This is called *electroluminescence.*

Other materials give off light when they are exposed to invisible radiation such as ultraviolet rays or electron beams. The screen of a TV tube is coated with such a *phosphor,* which lights up to make a picture when struck from inside the tube by a pattern of electrons.

What is light made of? In 1666 Sir Isaac Newton proposed a theory that light was similar to a stream of particles. This is called the particle or corpuscular theory. In 1864 James Clerk Maxwell stated that light waves were electromagnetic waves. The present-day the-

✳ THINGS TO DO

IN WHAT DIRECTION DOES LIGHT TRAVEL?

1 Cut a hole through the middle of three pieces of cardboard or some other stiff paper. Stand the pieces upright about a foot apart on a table, lined so that they are in a straight line and so that you can see straight through the holes.

2 Light a candle and place it at the end of the table opposite from where you are standing.

3 Look through the hole to see if the candle can be seen. Move one of the pieces to one side.

4 What happens? What does this tell you about the direction in which light travels?

✳ THINGS TO DO

HOW CAN YOU PREVENT TOTAL REFLECTION OF LIGHT?

1 Shine a light into the top of a jar of clear water. Notice how bright it is in the water yet the outside is dark.

2 Add a few drops of milk to the water and stir. Shine the light into the jar again. This time it appears less bright inside the jar and considerably lighter on the outside of the jar.

3 In the clear water the light hits the jar at such a small angle that total reflection occurs. By adding other particles to the water the light hits these and are reflected out through the glass.

---

ory is that light acts like both particles and waves. The particles are called *photons* and are given off by electrons that are going into lower energy orbits around their atom's nucleus. The regular rate at which these photons are given off by the atom is similar to the regular spacing of waves on water.

The color of light depends on the rate at which these photons leave the atom. Photons travel at one speed in a given material. The rate at which they leave must then affect only the spacing between photons or waves. This spacing is called *wavelength*. The rate is called FREQUENCY. The widest spaced, lowest frequency photons are called red light. The closest spaced, highest frequency photons are called violet light. All other visible colors are

between these. Invisible rays include the infrared (below the red) such as heat rays. Another invisible ray is the ultraviolet (above the violet) which causes suntan on our skin.

White light is emitted from a source where electrons are extremely active in a complex of orbital shifts. Thus, white light is made of a number of wave lengths. Certain shifts are characteristic in some materials which has radiation of only particular wave lengths. These produce bright SPECTRUM color lines. For example, heated sodium metal gives not white light but a bright yellow.

Invisible ultraviolet light possesses high energy. Fluorescent materials, when struck by this energy, soak it in, thus raising the levels of their electrons. But the electrons

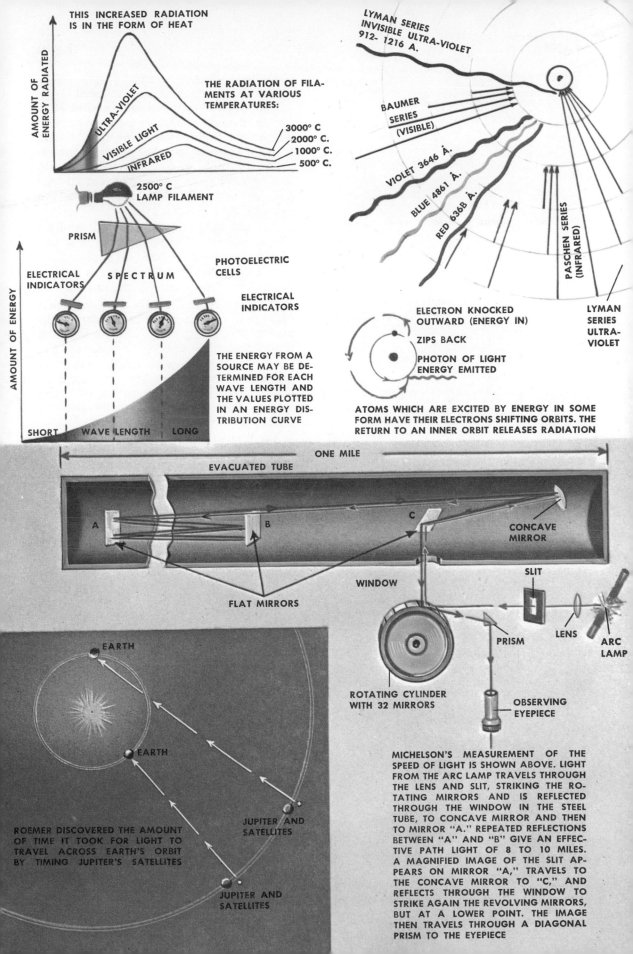

THIS INCREASED RADIATION IS IN THE FORM OF HEAT

AMOUNT OF ENERGY RADIATED

THE RADIATION OF FILA-MENTS AT VARIOUS TEMPERATURES:

3000° C
2000° C.
1000° C.
500° C.

ULTRA-VIOLET

VISIBLE LIGHT

INFRARED

2500° C LAMP FILAMENT

PRISM

ELECTRICAL INDICATORS

SPECTRUM

PHOTOELECTRIC CELLS

ELECTRICAL INDICATORS

AMOUNT OF ENERGY

SHORT   WAVE LENGTH   LONG

THE ENERGY FROM A SOURCE MAY BE DE-TERMINED FOR EACH WAVE LENGTH AND THE VALUES PLOTTED IN AN ENERGY DIS-TRIBUTION CURVE

LYMAN SERIES INVISIBLE ULTRA-VIOLET 912- 1216 A.

BAUMER SERIES (VISIBLE)

VIOLET 3646 Å.

BLUE 4861 Å.

RED 636B Å.

PASCHEN SERIES (INFRARED)

LYMAN SERIES ULTRA-VIOLET

ELECTRON KNOCKED OUTWARD (ENERGY IN)

ZIPS BACK

PHOTON OF LIGHT ENERGY EMITTED

ATOMS WHICH ARE EXCITED BY ENERGY IN SOME FORM HAVE THEIR ELECTRONS SHIFTING ORBITS. THE RETURN TO AN INNER ORBIT RELEASES RADIATION

ONE MILE

EVACUATED TUBE

A   B   C

CONCAVE MIRROR

FLAT MIRRORS

WINDOW

SLIT

PRISM

LENS

ARC LAMP

ROTATING CYLINDER WITH 32 MIRRORS

OBSERVING EYEPIECE

EARTH

EARTH

JUPITER AND SATELLITES

JUPITER AND SATELLITES

ROEMER DISCOVERED THE AMOUNT OF TIME IT TOOK FOR LIGHT TO TRAVEL ACROSS EARTH'S ORBIT BY TIMING JUPITER'S SATELLITES

MICHELSON'S MEASUREMENT OF THE SPEED OF LIGHT IS SHOWN ABOVE. LIGHT FROM THE ARC LAMP TRAVELS THROUGH THE LENS AND SLIT, STRIKING THE RO-TATING MIRRORS AND IS REFLECTED THROUGH THE WINDOW IN THE STEEL TUBE, TO CONCAVE MIRROR AND THEN TO MIRROR "A." REPEATED REFLECTIONS BETWEEN "A" AND "B" GIVE AN EFFEC-TIVE PATH LIGHT OF 8 TO 10 MILES. A MAGNIFIED IMAGE OF THE SLIT AP-PEARS ON MIRROR "A," TRAVELS TO THE CONCAVE MIRROR TO "C," AND REFLECTS THROUGH THE WINDOW TO STRIKE AGAIN THE REVOLVING MIRRORS, BUT AT A LOWER POINT. THE IMAGE THEN TRAVELS THROUGH A DIAGONAL PRISM TO THE EYEPIECE

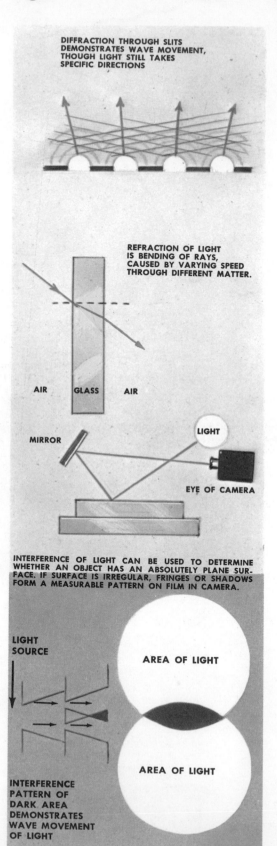

DIFFRACTION THROUGH SLITS DEMONSTRATES WAVE MOVEMENT, THOUGH LIGHT STILL TAKES SPECIFIC DIRECTIONS

REFRACTION OF LIGHT IS BENDING OF RAYS, CAUSED BY VARYING SPEED THROUGH DIFFERENT MATTER.

AIR   GLASS   AIR

MIRROR

LIGHT

EYE OF CAMERA

INTERFERENCE OF LIGHT CAN BE USED TO DETERMINE WHETHER AN OBJECT HAS AN ABSOLUTELY PLANE SURFACE. IF SURFACE IS IRREGULAR, FRINGES OR SHADOWS FORM A MEASURABLE PATTERN ON FILM IN CAMERA.

LIGHT SOURCE

AREA OF LIGHT

AREA OF LIGHT

INTERFERENCE PATTERN OF DARK AREA DEMONSTRATES WAVE MOVEMENT OF LIGHT

U.V. light. Instead longer visible waves (lower-energy photons) are released.

The speed of light was measured in 1676 by Ole Roemer, a Danish astronomer, who noticed the differences in the time it took for light to cross the solar system from Jupiter. The *speed of light,* given the symbol c, is 186,281 miles per second. (In kilometers per second, 299,792.8). This is the speed of light in a VACUUM.

As light travels from a source, the light falls in intensity. The illumination at a surface is expressed by the INVERSE-SQUARE LAW. Light intensity falls off, not as the distance, but as the *square* of the distance.

Newton's corpuscular theory helps to explain reflection. It might be similar to the way in which ping pong balls bounce from a surface that is smooth or irregular. *Refraction* of ball particles can be shown in a model having two surfaces connected by a slope. The ball is "shoved" in the same way as light is refracted as it enters or leaves glass from air.

The particle model gets complicated in order to explain the happenings of reflection and refraction at a surface at the same time. The model fails in making refraction take place as it might with the ball on the sloping surface. It would be necessary for light to travel faster in the material doing the refracting rather than the dense air or the vacuum. This would mean that the speed of light in water would be $\frac{4}{3}$ that of in air, or $1\frac{1}{3}$ time faster. This cannot be proved.

A wave model for light shows that waves can pass through one another. Particles have a chance of colliding. Waves reflect at a boundary, and even partially when they meet a shallow boundary. The refraction of waves in a new direction takes place when a shallower portion of a tank is met.

A wave model can show *diffraction*. This is an effect of light bending around corners. A tank in which a lens-shaped shallow portion is set will illustrate either a convex or concave lens.

Interference of light occurs when waves either cancel one another or produce a double crest.

Light is measured by a photoelectric meter. Light energy striking the surface of specially-treated substances will cause a flow of electrons which will be circuited through a galvanometer. The units for measuring

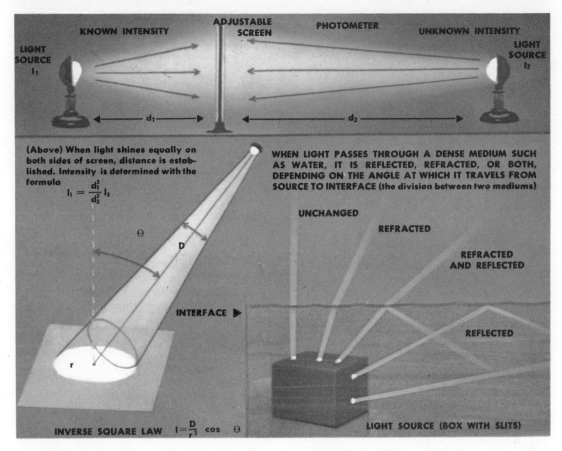

KNOWN INTENSITY   ADJUSTABLE SCREEN   PHOTOMETER   UNKNOWN INTENSITY

LIGHT SOURCE I_1 LIGHT SOURCE I_2

d_1 d_2

(Above) When light shines equally on both sides of screen, distance is established. Intensity is determined with the formula

$$I_1 = \frac{d_1^2}{d_2^2} I_2$$

WHEN LIGHT PASSES THROUGH A DENSE MEDIUM SUCH AS WATER, IT IS REFLECTED, REFRACTED, OR BOTH, DEPENDING ON THE ANGLE AT WHICH IT TRAVELS FROM SOURCE TO INTERFACE (the division between two mediums)

UNCHANGED

REFRACTED

REFRACTED AND REFLECTED

θ

D

INTERFACE ▶

REFLECTED

r

INVERSE SQUARE LAW $I = \dfrac{D}{r^2} \cos \theta$ LIGHT SOURCE (BOX WITH SLITS)

light intensity are called *lumens* or *foot-candles*. Light can be converted directly to electrical energy in SOLAR CELLS.

Life is dependent upon light. Without the trapping and storing by CHLOROPHYLL in living plants of light energy, H_2O, and CO_2 (for forming sugars) there would be no chain of life. All life depends on this process of PHOTOSYNTHESIS.   F. R. W.
SEE ALSO: CANDLEPOWER, DISPERSION, ELECTROMAGNETIC SPECTRUM, LIGHT YEAR, LUMINESCENCE, MIRROR, PHOTOCHEMISTRY, PHOTOELECTRICITY, RADIATION, SUN

Light year In measuring the distance from one star to another, or from Earth to a star, the usual units of measurement, such as miles, are far too small. In order to keep the number of digits in the measurement of these distances to a reasonable amount, the VELOCITY of light is employed. A light year is the total distance that light will travel in one year.

Since the velocity of light is about 2.99 x 10^8 meters per second (or about 186,000 miles per second), the distance in terms of meters for one light year is approximately 924 x 10^{13} meters (9,240,000,000,000,000 meters). In terms of miles it is 573 x 10^{10} miles (5,730,000,000,000 miles).   A. E. L.
SEE ALSO: LIGHT, STAR

Lightning Lightning is the bright flash of light which is often seen during storms. The flash is actually a discharge of ELECTRICITY in the air. THUNDER is a familiar result of the discharge.

When certain conditions occur in the ATMOSPHERE, clouds will accumulate an electric charge. Clouds may gather this charge from coming into contact with layers of charged air or by the falling of charged rain drops. Because a group of CLOUDS is charged with either negative or positive electricity, an excess opposite charge accumulates on the ground below the clouds or in a cluster of nearby clouds. An electric

✳ THINGS TO DO

HOW FAR AWAY FROM YOU IS A THUNDERSTORM?

1 Watch the sky during a thunderstorm. The second you see the lightning start counting off the seconds—by saying "one thousand and one, one thousand and two, one thousand and three, etc.", until you hear the clap of thunder.

2 If you have counted up to five seconds (one thousand and five) the center of the storm is one mile away. If you reach thirty seconds, the lightning is six miles away.

3 By counting periodically you will be able to tell whether the storm is coming toward you or going in the opposite direction by the decreasing or increasing number of seconds.

4 Sound travels about one-fifth mile per second and light travels 186,000 miles per second.

field is produced between the cloud and the earth, or between the groups of clouds. When this field becomes strong enough, an electric discharge will take place. This discharge is lightning. This discharge is similar to the spark one experiences when touching a metal object after walking across a wool carpet.   A. E. L.
SEE ALSO: CLOUDS, ELECTRICITY, THUNDERSTORM, WEATHER, WEATHER FORECASTING

Lignite see Coal

F. A. Blashfield
Lilac bush

Lilac (LYE-lack) Lilac is a shrub of the SYRINGA family. It is known for its fragrant flowers that appear in the spring. Many towns have lilac festivals at the time of lilac blooming. The flowers grow as *panicles,* which means a cluster of tiny flowers, with longer floral stems at the base of the cluster. These flowers range in color from white through purple. Because the most common color is a lavender, lilac has become another name for a light purple color.

Lilac bushes are easily grown and need only occasional pruning or thinning out. Numerous varieties of French hybrid lilacs have been developed which some consider superior to the common lilac. They bloom earlier and have larger flowers although some are not as fragrant as the common lilac. The plant is propagated by seed, layering, suckers, and grafting. GRAFTING is done on both lilac and privet stock, but the privet is less satisfactory. The maximum height of the many lilacs varies from six to thirty feet.   J. A. D.
SEE ALSO: PROPAGATION

Lily Lily is the common name of a large family of plants. They are a favorite and important garden plant. Lilies usually have large, elegant, fragrant flowers. They are PERENNIALS and grow from a scaly BULB. They grow in full sun or partial shade, according to the variety. Lilies need heavy fertilization to produce their showiest flowers. They bloom in late spring or summer.

Helen J. Challand

Calla lilies

Lily-of-the-valley

Lilies are bulbous herbs of the family *Liliaceae. Lilium* is the old Latin name of the lilies. The flower parts are typically in sixes. The flowers are erect, nodding or horizontal, and grow in clusters or singly. They must be replanted often to keep a good supply in the garden, and they require special care. Bulb-rooting lilies produce roots from the base of the bulb and require shallow planting. Stem-rooting lilies develop feeding roots along the stem between the bulb and the surface of the bulb, and need deep planting. Lilies must have a year-round MULCH, preferably dried leaves. To insure a particular color, or size, a variety of lily bulbs should be planted.

Raising lilies from seed provides a large number of bulbs but may result in a variation of type. It takes from two to four years for lilies raised from seed to flower. The foliage dies after blooming, and lilies may then be lifted, divided, and re-planted. They should be replanted at once to prevent drying out. One bulb with mosaic, a VIRUS disease of lilies, can infect all the others. Diseased bulbs should be destroyed. Such lilies as the Easter lily are usually forced in greenhouses.

Best known members of the lily family are the *regal* from China; the *tiger,* a native of China and Korea; and the *Madonna* lily from southern Europe. From some of these have been developed the hybrid Mariposa and Gloriosa.   M. R. L.

Lily-of-the-valley Lily-of-the-valley is a spring blooming flower that is easy to grow. These flowers prefer shady spots and will often grow in places where no other flowers can live.

Lily-of-the-valley grows about eight inches tall. The leaves are thick and spiked. Sometimes the leaves almost cover the delicate flowers. The flowers are usually white, although some are pink. They look like little bells growing on slender stalks and are sweet-smelling. They are often used in bridal bouquets.

The plants are multiplied by root division. *Pips* that develop on the roots form the new plants.   M. R. L.

Lima bean see Legume

Lime (chemical) Lime is a term referring to both calcium oxide—*quicklime*—and calcium hydroxide—*slaked lime*. Both are made from limestone treated to remove CO_2 (carbon dioxide). Lime is used in the building and other industries and in water treatment.
SEE: ROCKS

Lime (fruit) see Citrus fruit

Limpet (LIMM-pet) A limpet is a small, flat-shelled sea animal. Different species live along rocky shores of all oceans. They eat seaweed, using their rasping tongues. A few kinds are eaten by man. Some limpets have shells with heavy ribs.

Limpets are *mollusks*. Their flat shells are shaped like lopsided cups, but their internal

Limpets

Buchsbaum

organs are twisted in a spiral during the larval stages, showing their relation to other *gastropods,* such as snails. Limpets can tighten their shells snugly against their rock footing and so avoid injury from their enemies. The *keyhole limpet* is peculiar in having a round opening in the middle of its shell. Most limpets are only about two inches long. They may live 10 to 12 years.   D. A. B.

SEE ALSO: MOLLUSCA

Linden tree
Courtesy Society For
Visual Education, Inc.

Linden Basswood is another name for this shade tree. It may grow over 120 feet tall. Leaves are simple and heart-shaped. The flowers are yellow and the fruit is dry.

The wood is one of the softest, lightest, and weakest of all other hardwoods. Strong fibers in the xylem are called *bast* fibers. The LEAVES are alternate, serrate, and have pinnate venation. Each FLOWER of the inflorescence has five petals and sepals, numerous stamens, and a pistil of five carpels. Dry capsules hang down from a long modified leaf or bract. This acts like a propeller in whirling the FRUIT to the ground. Linden belongs to family Tiliaceae.   H. J. C.

Linear accelerator see Accelerators (particle)

Linear venation see Leaves

Linen Linen is a fabric or yarn made from *flax.* Flax is the earliest vegetable fiber ever used. Linen 5,000 years old has been found in Egyptian tombs. All through history, linen has been used throughout the world. Today, Ireland is the chief producer of linen. The finest flax fiber is from Belgium.

U. S. Department of Agriculture photo
Flax fibers are made into linen

The best linen yarn must be made by hand. Because of high labor costs in the United States, very little linen is produced. France, Germany, England, and the Netherlands are large producers of flax.

Before being made into cloth, the flax must go through a number of processes. Toward the end of August, when the flax is a light brown color, the farmer harvests it. After the stalks are tied into bundles and dried thoroughly in the sun, they are passed through a coarse comb which separates the seeds from the stalks. This is called *rippling*. Next comes the *retting* process, which means the plants are kept moist and bacterial decomposition of many of the cells of the stem loosens the fine linen fibers. Then the plants are dried again; this is called *grassing*. After grassing, the stalks are put through a *scutching* machine which removes the woody portions from the fibrous. The final step is *hackling* (heckling), which is another combing process to separate the best of the flax. For the finest linen, hackling must be done again and again, using finer and finer combs.

The beauty of linen consists in the evenness of the thread. Linen with a round thread is considered better than that with a flat thread.

The heaviest linens are made into tents, sailcloth, canvas, carpets, and carpet backings. Medium-weights include crash, ticking, sheeting, duck, and art linens. The finest linens are used for handkerchiefs, tablecloths, and fine clothing.   J. K. K.

Carolus Linnaeus

Linnaeus, Carolus (lih-NEE-us, KARE-uh-luhs) (1707-1778) Carolus Linnaeus was a Swedish botanist who first classified plants by giving them a double Latin name. The first name was the genus, and the first letter was capitalized. The second name was the species, and the first letter was not capitalized. This two-name method of naming is called *binomial, bi* meaning "two." For example, Linnaeus put the flower known as the *primrose* into a genus he called *Primula*. One kind of primrose with purple flowers he called *Primula versus*. Thus Linnaeus was able to classify and name thousands of plants. Believing that everything in nature could be classified if the scientist had the time and patience, Linnaeus also began to classify animals in the same way.

Of his 180 books, Linnaeus' first, *Systema Naturae,* was the most important. It contained only twelve pages, but it marked the beginning of modern BOTANY. In it he dealt with the sex and reproduction of plants, a field never before explored.

Born in Rashult, Sweden, Linnaeus was the son of a village clergyman. His name originally was Carl von Linné, but he later took the Latin form of his name. A poor grammar-school student, Linnaeus could not decide what he wanted to do with his life. He was educated at great personal expense to his impoverished father, but he finally was graduated from the University of Uppsala and began to distinguish himself in botany until he finally became professor of botany and director of the university botanical gardens. An extremely popular teacher, he had huge classes of several hundred students from all over the world.

World famous, Linnaeus was one of the best loved and most highly respected professional men of his day. In fact, he was the first scientist ever to be made a noble in the country of Sweden.   D. H. J.

SEE ALSO: ANIMALS, CLASSIFICATION OF; PLANTS, CLASSIFICATION OF

Linnet

Linnet The linnet is a small (5½″) sparrow-like songbird common over Europe and Asia. There are some varieties in North America. It is related to and looks like a FINCH—fluffy, brownish-red with dark streaking on its sides and a small either red or gray crest. It flocks in large numbers, eats seeds, and nests in evergreens.

Linseed oil Linseed oil is a yellow oil made by crushing the seeds of blue-flowered FLAX. It is used as a drying oil in manufacturing paint and in making linoleum and printing inks.

Linseed oil forms a rubbery film upon exposure to air, so-called *drying*. It is this film mixed with cork that is spread on burlap to make linoleum. Likewise, this rubbery skin gives the paint which contains linseed oil a durable, weather resistant quality.   J. M. C.

Lion see Cat family

Lipase see Digestive system, Liver

Liquid Without liquid, life as we know it on Earth would be impossible. Space travelers could not live on the moon or planets if there were no liquids there or if they could not bring enough with them.

Liquids are necessary for both plants and animals. Both blood, which is a liquid, and sap, another liquid, carry nourishment through the bodies of animals and through the stems and leaves of plants. Without this nourishment they would die.

Without liquids there would be no oceans, no running brooks, no lakes and no rain.

All matter has three conditions. It may be a *gas,* it may take the form of a *solid,* or, finally, it may be a flowing *liquid.*

Those who have seen water turn to ice or have watched steam pour from a kettle know that matter which is normally liquid may become either a solid or a gas. However, matter is called liquid if that is its normal form under ordinary conditions of temperature. In many cases, also, conditions of pressure may change liquid to another form.

Modern-day scientists have even been able to make normally solid matter assume liquid form. Such is the case in some of the new processes for turning coal into liquid, at normal temperatures.

The small "pieces" which go together to form all matter are known as *molecules.* These are held together by an action called *cohesion.* Cohesion is strongest in solids; the greater the cohesion the more "solid" the matter.

Liquids are "liquid" because their cohesion is less. Their molecules can move about to a greater degree than in solids, and so they flow into a container and take its form.

Some liquids flow less readily than others. "Slow as molasses in January" is a familiar phrase which illustrates this point. The

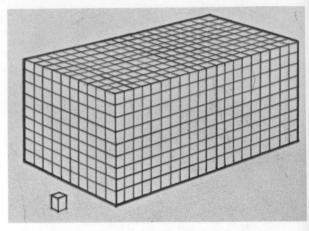

ONE VOLUME OF LIQUID WATER (H_2O) EXPANDS TO 1800 VOLUMES IN STEAM

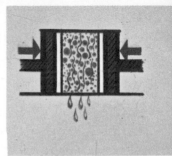

A GAS, SUCH AS WATER VAPOR, CAN BE COMPRESSED TO FORM A LIQUID. THIS PRINCIPLE IS OFTEN USED IN REFRIGERATION.

LIQUID WILL EQUALIZE ITS LEVEL OR LEVELS, REGARDLESS OF SHAPE OF CONTAINER

slower flowing liquids are called *viscous.* The molecules in viscous liquids are more tightly bound together, giving the appearance and action of the popular term "sticky."

As far as is known, there are no completely *nonviscous* liquids. Helium, chilled almost to absolute zero, is thought to be the most nearly nonviscous liquid. A liquid which was entirely nonviscous would be called an "ideal" liquid.

In an absolutely weight-free state, a

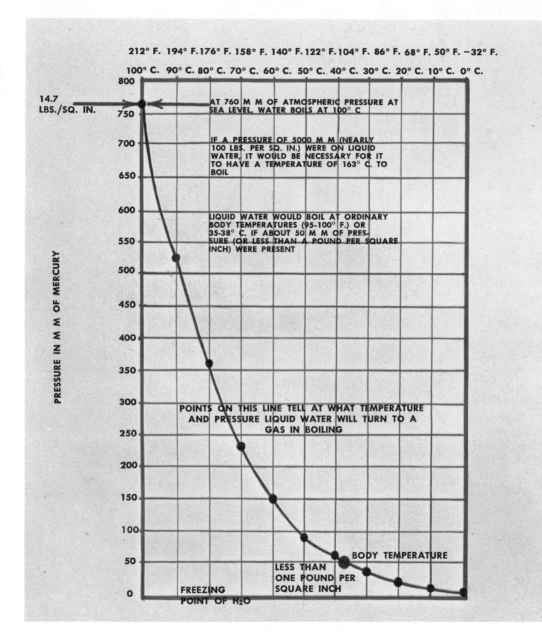

Liquid is one of the states in which matter can exist. The properties of liquids have been described in many physical principles

quantity of liquid would assume the shape of a ball. The molecules tend to hold a liquid together at the surface. This holding power of the molecules has been given the name SURFACE TENSION. Because of surface tension, liquid suspended in space, completely without gravity, would hold together in the form of a sphere, just as a drop of water does as it appears to stick and hang from a water tap.

The drop is held together by surface ten-

sion until enough water has accumulated to increase the weight. When the weight becomes too heavy, the surface tension can no longer hold the little sphere of water together, and it drops from the faucet.

Those who have observed insects apparently walking along the surface of water were noting an example of the surface tension of water. The insect was being supported by what Professor Charles Vernon Boys called "an elastic skin of water."

This skin of surface tension is strong enough sometimes even to support metal objects, such as foil, on water.

Sometimes the molecules of a liquid seem to be pulled toward various solids. Different kinds of liquids behave differently in this regard.

If a hollow straw of glass not much larger than a hair were placed in a container of water, the water would rise in the straw to a considerable height. The force which causes this is called *capillary action*. It was given this name because such a hollow straw is very much like a hair, and the Latin word for hair is *capillus*.

Molecules within a liquid are not stationary. They move about continually in all directions. When a molecule of liquid has gained enough force to push itself through the surface tension, it leaves the main body of the liquid. When this occurs, the process is known as EVAPORATION. Higher temperatures cause the molecules to have greater speed and energy, and more of them will escape from the surface tension as the temperature rises. The hot sun beating down on a small quantity of water will cause all of its molecules to move faster and fly away or evaporate.

These escaped molecules are given the name *vapor*. As the temperature cools, the molecules lose some of their energy and begin to pull back together in small drops. If the process continues, the smaller drops also come together, and the liquid form is resumed. CONDENSATION is the term given to this action.

Very rapid heating of a liquid makes the molecules move with great speed and vigor. Many of them come together at once and push their way to the surface in a bubble, and we say the liquid is *boiling*. When this occurs, the liquid is said to have reached the BOILING POINT.

Various liquids behave differently when brought into contact with solids. Sometimes the liquid will spread out and cover the solid. Liquids are said to have greater *adhesion* to those solids over which they spread easily.

On other solids the same liquid will simply stay in small beads over the surface.

Although water has great adhesion with clean glass, a film of oily material spread over the glass would cause water to pull together in drops. Oil and water remain

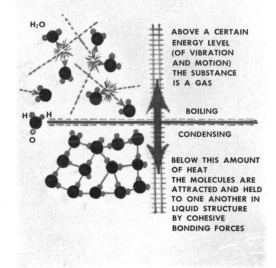

A VAPOR CONDENSING TO A LIQUID HAS MOLECULES OF LESS ENERGY (HEAT). AS ITS MOLECULES COME CLOSE TOGETHER FOR COHESIVE FORCE TO CAUSE THEM TO REMAIN TOGETHER AND NOT BOUND APART AS THEY DO IN GAS

H_2O

ABOVE A CERTAIN ENERGY LEVEL (OF VIBRATION AND MOTION) THE SUBSTANCE IS A GAS

BOILING

CONDENSING

BELOW THIS AMOUNT OF HEAT THE MOLECULES ARE ATTRACTED AND HELD TO ONE ANOTHER IN LIQUID STRUCTURE BY COHESIVE BONDING FORCES

Molecules of matter in the liquid state can exchange bonds and readily shift about, giving it the fluid property

separate because they have almost no adhesion.

Many chemicals can be dissolved in liquids to give molecules more adhesion, reducing their surface tension. These chemicals are called *wetting agents* or DETERGENTS. Popular cleaning materials today act as wetting agents, bringing water into closer contact with the solids which are soiling the push their way to the surface in a bubble, objects to be cleaned. They can then be moved off the surface more easily.   J. A. C.

SEE ALSO: ADHESION, CAPILLARITY, FREEZING POINT, OSMOSIS, PHYSICAL STATES AND CHANGES, VAPOR PRESSURE

Liquid air Liquid air is ordinary air which has been made into a liquid by compressing and cooling it. It looks much like water but has a temperature of minus 312°F., so cold that it boils when brought into contact with ice. It is used in REFRIGERATION.

Lister, Joseph (1827-1912) Lister was a British surgeon who discovered how to use antiseptics to kill harmful germs. Before Lister experimented with carbolic acid and learned to sterilize with it, many people died from simple wounds or surgery. He showed doctors the need to fight germs.

Born at Upton, in Essex, Lister was the son of a wine merchant who studied optics in his spare time and whose work on the achromatic lens (the lens that refracts light without breaking it into its constituent colors) and the compound microscope opened the door to a fellowship in the Royal Society. Like his father, young Lister loved science.

Lister was a brilliant medical student and at the age of twenty-five was a fellow of the Royal College of Surgeons. Studying under Professor William Sharpey and Dr. James Syme, two of the leading surgeons of all Europe, Joseph Lister distinguished himself both professionally and personally. Eventually, however, he was to surpass his famous teachers.

When Lister was twenty-nine, he married Agnes Syme, oldest daughter of Dr. Syme. During the almost forty years of their marriage she was by his side constantly, helping as secretary, research assistant, attendant, and wife.

It is difficult to fully appreciate the gift Joseph Lister gave to the world. When he first studied surgery, far more patients died than lived. Although surgeons were skillful in performing operations, a few days later infections would set in and the wounds would begin to putrefy. Dr. Lister began to suspect that this putrefaction was carried into the wounds by the air. Then one of his friends called his attention to the work on fermentation done by LOUIS PASTEUR, who had shown that fermentation of wine was caused by bacteria from the air. This was the answer, Lister reasoned, but how could the germs be destroyed?

Soon he learned that a chemist named Calvert had used carbolic acid to disinfect sewage, and he wondered if it might not serve the purpose of the surgeon. After considerable research, Lister discovered that he could use a diluted solution and it would not harm body tissues. In addition, it would effectively sterilize surgical instruments. He had to subject his theory to tests, and he was highly gratified to discover that of the eleven patients on whom he had used ANTISEPTICS, only one had died.   D. H. J.

Liter see Measurement

Lithium Lithium is the lightest metallic element known. It was discovered in 1817 by a Swedish chemist, J. A. Arfvedson. It is a silver-white metal that tarnishes easily.

Lithium is found for the most part in North America and Africa and is mined with pegmatite (granite) ores.

In industry, it is used in manufacturing glass and ceramic products and in lubricants. It can easily be worked, extruded or drawn and so may be used for delicate parts.

The atomic number of lithium (symbol Li) is 3; its atomic weight is 6.940 (6.939 since 1961); its boiling point is 1200°C. and melting point is 180°C.   D. A. B.
SEE ALSO: ELEMENTS

Lithography see Printing

Lithophyte see Lichen, Marine biology

Litmus test The litmus test is a way of testing the acidity or alkalinity of a solution. Filter paper saturated with a solution of litmus and dried turns red in acid and blue in a base (alkali).
SEE: ACIDS AND BASES

Litmus test for acids and bases

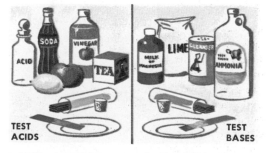

Little America see Antarctica

Little Dipper see Big and Little Dippers, Ursa Major and Ursa Minor

Live oak see Oak

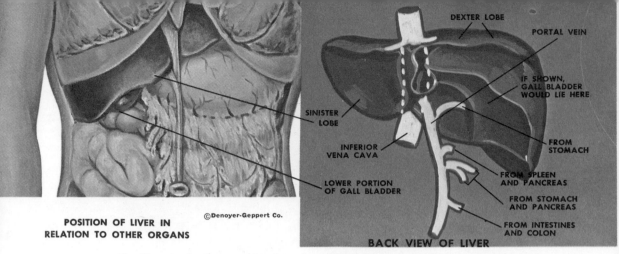

POSITION OF LIVER IN
RELATION TO OTHER ORGANS

©Denoyer-Geppert Co.

DEXTER LOBE

PORTAL VEIN

IF SHOWN,
GALL BLADDER
WOULD LIE HERE

SINISTER
LOBE

INFERIOR
VENA CAVA

FROM
STOMACH

LOWER PORTION
OF GALL BLADDER

FROM SPLEEN
AND PANCREAS

FROM STOMACH
AND PANCREAS

FROM INTESTINES
AND COLON

BACK VIEW OF LIVER

The liver is the largest gland in the body. It is used mainly in digestion

Liver This organ, because it performs so many tasks, is often called the "warehouse" or "clearing house" for the body. All digested food passes from the digestive tract through the circulatory system to the liver. The liver may break it down into simpler compounds and from these build new substances useful in the body. For example, fatty acids (from the digestion of fats) may be broken down and made into carbohydrates. The reverse of this process may also take place.

The liver is the largest digestive organ in the human body, weighing about three pounds. It lies toward the right and beneath the diaphragm, or the sheet of MUSCLE under the *lung*. True livers are in all vertebrates; invertebrate "livers" digest and absorb.

One function of the liver is making and secreting bile. Bile is composed of salts, water, and such compounds as *lecithin* and *cholesterol*. Usually, bile is stored in a sac or GALLBLADDER before being released into the small intestine by way of the bile duct. Gallbladders are present in most vertebrates. Horses, rats, and deer lack them and it may or may not occur in giraffes. In the gallbladder, bile is concentrated by water absorption. Mucus and bile pigments are added. The pigments are wastes from the breakdown of worn red blood cells by the liver. These are added to digestive wastes in the large intestine.

Bile breaks up (emulsifies) fat particles in the intestine so that fat digesting enzymes can function. After fats have been digested, bile salts are absorbed in the posterior end of the small intestine and returned to the liver. Back in the liver, they stimulate the production of more bile.

The liver acts as a storehouse for vitamins A, D, B_{12}, and folic acid. It also stores iron, recovered from the destruction of worn out red blood cells, copper, and glycogen, made from digested sugar.

Waste materials in the large intestine are concentrated by the absorption of excess water. The water is sent to the liver where liver cells detoxify it and release any excess into the bloodstream to be excreted by the kidneys. Cells in the liver, Kupffer cells, engulf and digest foreign materials such as bacteria and parts of old red blood cells. This process is called *phagocytosis*.

Most of the plasma proteins in blood are made in the liver. Examples are prothrombin and fibrinogen. Both of these are important in blood clotting. Albumin, which helps control plasma volume by taking water out of tissues, is also important.

In blood, the level of sugar (in the form of glucose) is about 0.1%. The liver helps to maintain this level by changing stored glycogen back into glucose and releasing it into the bloodstream, or by the reverse reaction.

Much of the metabolism (use) of fatty acids and amino acids is determined in the liver. Fatty acids may be released to the blood for cellular use, changed to sugar and stored as glycogen, or remade into the specific fat of the organism and stored as adipose tissue.

Amino acids may be sent to cells for making protein, or their nitrogens may be removed, changed to urea, and sent to the kidneys for excretion. The rest of the molecule may be made into sugar, glycogen, or fat.

J. C. K.

SEE ALSO: DIGESTIVE SYSTEM, VITAMINS

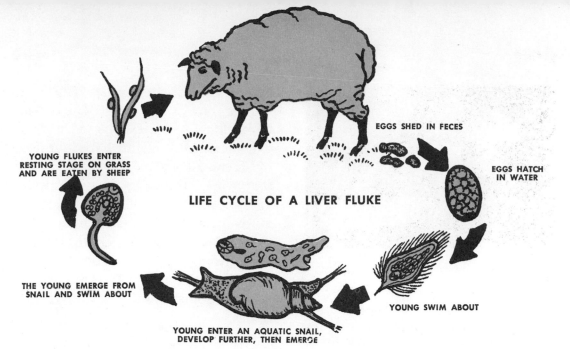

YOUNG FLUKES ENTER RESTING STAGE ON GRASS AND ARE EATEN BY SHEEP

EGGS SHED IN FECES

EGGS HATCH IN WATER

LIFE CYCLE OF A LIVER FLUKE

THE YOUNG EMERGE FROM SNAIL AND SWIM ABOUT

YOUNG SWIM ABOUT

YOUNG ENTER AN AQUATIC SNAIL, DEVELOP FURTHER, THEN EMERGE

Liver fluke The liver fluke is a leaf-shaped flatworm about one-half to one inch long. It is common in Japan and China. The adult lives as a parasite in the bile duct of the human LIVER. Between the egg and the adult stages, there are four kinds of young (LARVAE). Two of these must develop inside a snail and two in a fish.

The liver fluke is covered by a tough *cuticula* and has two suckers with which to cling to its host. It has a well-developed digestive system, with a short muscular esophagus which divides into two long unbranched intestines (intestinal caeca).

The flatworm is *hermaphroditic,* which means that both female ovaries and male testes are present in the same animal. However, there is cross-fertilization. There are two testes, one on each side of the body. Two tubes, *vas deferens,* run from each testis and unite to form a sperm duct (*seminal vesicle*). The sperm duct is attached to a penis which may be pushed out through an opening called the *genital pore.*

Eggs are produced in a single ovary from which a short tube or *oviduct* leads to the shell gland. Yolk glands in the body also connect to the shell gland. The shell gland opens into an organ known as the *seminal receptacle.*

The eggs containing a complete larva, the *miracidium,* leave the human body in the feces (waste material from the large intestine). They do not hatch unless eaten by a snail. In the snail, the miracidia change into *sporocysts* which produces a generation of larvae called *rediae.* The rediae pass into the liver and develop into tadpole-like *cercariae* larvae. These leave the snail and swim about until they meet the right species of fish. The cercaria bore into the body of the fish, lose their tails, and, as *metacercariae,* encyst in the muscles. If man eats raw infected fish, the cysts dissolves in the stomach and frees the metacercariae, which migrate to the bile duct and become adults.   J. C. K.

SEE ALSO: PARASITE, PLATYHELMINTHES, REPRODUCTIVE SYSTEMS

Liverworts Liverworts are close relatives of the mosses. They both belong to an important group of simple plants, the phylum *Bryophyta.* They are very small individually, but because of the great number of species (over 7,000) they form an important part of the vegetation in some parts of the world.

Liverworts live only in moist areas, such as cool woods. banks of streams and wet canyon walls.

Liverworts are divided according to their structure into two main groups. The *thallose* liverworts are always flattened. They may be simple and strap-like, branched, or in the form of rosettes. All grow flat against the

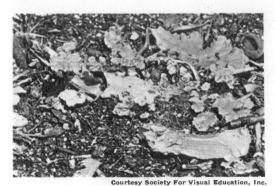
Courtesy Society For Visual Education, Inc.
Liverworts are simple plants

soil or rock. Many have rows of scales on the under surface. The internal structure may be very simple, or it may contain specialized air chambers which open to the upper surface through pores.

The *leafy* liverworts have a central stem with two rows of leaves arranged laterally along it, and sometimes with a third row of leaves along the under side. A common leafy liverwort is *Bazzania trilobata,* found in cool woods from Labrador to Florida, and west to the Mississippi River.

A common thallose liverwort is *Conocephalum conicum.* It grows in mats over muddy stream banks and moist canyon walls. If a bit of the thallus is crushed, it gives a pleasant, spicy odor.

All liverworts are excellent examples of the ALTERNATION OF GENERATIONS. The GAMETOPHYTE is the conspicuous part of the life cycle. Sperm and egg cells are produced in antheridia and archegonia on the gametophyte. Moisture is necessary for the sperm cells to reach the egg. The fertilized egg cell gives rise to the SPOROPHYTE which, in most cases, consists of a spore capsule and a slender, transparent stalk. Scattered in among the spores are usually found spiral structures (*elaters*) which aid in their dispersal. Liverworts often reproduce by vegetative means, that is, a portion of the plant body such as a leaf, branch or bud, may give rise to a new plant.

Despite their small size, liverworts play a part in the weathering of rock and in soil conservation. In places favorable to their growth, they make good ground cover, and prevent rapid run off of water.

Bryophytes may have evolved from some form of filamentous green algae as shown by the structures of forms living today. M. D. F.
SEE ALSO: BRYOPHYTES, SPORE FORMATION

Lizard Lizards are reptiles with long, slender bodies and tails. Their skin, which they shed frequently, is made of dry scales. Most lizards have four legs, but some have none. There are more than three thousand kinds (species and subspecies), and they are found all over the world, especially in warm areas. They vary in length from a little over an inch to about ten feet. There are about one hundred species of lizard found in southwestern United States.

Lizards and snakes are order *Squamata* in the reptile class of vertebrates. The lizards are in suborder *Sauria.* The bodies of most lizards found on land are flat from top to bottom (vertically). Those of water lizards are flat from side to side (horizontally), and those of burrowing lizards are usually round and snakelike. Many lizards are brightly colored and some are able to change certain colors quickly.

Lizards move in different ways. A few species have lost their legs as they evolved or else they have small, helpless legs. These kinds undulate like snakes and burrow into the ground. Those with four well-developed legs usually walk or run on all fours, though some of them rear up and run on their hind legs when they are really in a hurry. *Geckos* have pad-like disks with hooked hairs on their feet and can run up walls and even across ceilings. The so-called *flying dragons* have wing-like membranes which enable them to glide from tree to tree. A few lizards can swim, as the ancestors of all lizards probably did.

Some species of lizard lay eggs. Others bear live baby lizards. Mother lizards do not take care of their babies after they are born, though some of the egg-laying species protect the eggs from predators.

Lizards eat plants, insects, eggs, fishes, small birds and mammals, and just about anything they can catch and subdue. Usually they seize their food with their jaws, but some kinds, such as the *chameleons,* shoot out their long tongues to grab insects.

Lizards protect themselves in various ways. Only the GILA MONSTER and the *Mexican beaded lizard* have poisonous venom. Running away and hiding are usually the lizards' best defenses. Different species have various ways

Courtesy Society For Visual Education, Inc.

There are several thousand species of lizards; for example, the collared lizard with its distinctive markings (top); the glass snake, a legless lizard (center); and the tough-skinned horned toad (bottom)

of frightening or confusing their enemies. *Horned toads,* for example, are protected with spines and are able to squirt blood from their eyes into the face of the predator if they are attacked. The blood contains a substance that many mammals, such as coyotes and wolves, find very disagreeable. Some lizards have a trick of discarding their tails. Sometimes the tail is larger than the rest of the lizard and the enemy fights the tail while the lizard scoots away. It then grows a new tail; the new tail may not be as large or complete as the old. Some lizards hiss and puff up to frighten their enemies.

The legless *snake lizards* and *worm lizards* are apt to be mistaken for snakes and worms except by experts. D. A. B.

SEE ALSO: CHAMELEON, REPTILIA

Llama Though smaller than a camel, the llama is a member of the camel family. It is found in South America. Llamas do not have humps like camels, but they are used as beasts of burden. They can go for several days without water. They are sure-footed and used to living at high altitudes. They make good pack animals for mountainous areas.

Llama is the name given the domestic animals of the species. The wild relative is called the *guanaco.* South American Indians tamed the llama many centuries ago. Llamas are shaggy beasts and provide good wool for clothing. The *alpaca,* a variety of llama, is bred for its wool. The *vicuna* is a wild type that produces especially fine wool. The meat of the llama can be eaten. Llamas also produce milk, though it is not very tasty.

The llama is a stubborn animal. If it gets tired of carrying its load, it lies down. If its load happens to be human, it might well twist its long neck, face the rider, and spit a very unpleasant-smelling shower of saliva into the rider's face. C. L. K.

Llama

Loam Loam is a fertile soil. It consists of CLAY, enough sand so the clay does not stick together, a trace of lime, and decayed animal or vegetable matter called HUMUS.

SEE: SOIL TYPES

Purple-flowered lobelia (left) and cardinal flower (right), the only red lobelia

Lobelia (loh-BEEL-yuh) Lobelia is any of the large group of flowers with clusters of beautiful red, white, or blue tubular blooms split on the upper side. They are mostly ANNUAL plants and are widely grown for ornamental purposes. The most common species in North America is called *Indian tobacco*. Indians used it for medicine.

Lobster These are large, saltwater animals very much like the freshwater crayfish. They belong to the order Decapoda because they have ten legs. Lobsters may live to be about 50 years old and weigh 35 to 40 pounds. The first pair of legs is for defense, and is a large pair of pincers (chelipeds). An outside skeleton with jointed legs places the lobster in the phylum ARTHROPODA.

Lobsters belong to the class CRUSTACEA because they have gills for breathing and very hard outer, or *exoskeletons,* made of CHITIN and lime salts. Bodies are divided into a head and thorax of fused segments, or joints, and a segmented abdomen. Organ systems for digestion, circulation, coordination, excretion, sensation, and reproduction are very similar to those of the CRAYFISH.

Many lobsters dig burrows in the sand with their first three pair of legs. Excavated material is carried to the surface by the pincers. Burrows have two entrances with rooms large enough for turning around. Some lobsters use natural retreats such as rock or coral crevices or sheltered areas under ledges.

These crustaceans feed on any animal they can catch and kill with their pincers. Mollusks, fish, and other crustaceans of appropriate size are eaten. They are also *scavengers*

Buchsbaum

American lobster

feeding on dead animals and plants. Food is passed by the pincers to the food-handling mouth parts, the three pairs of maxillipeds, and first pair of *maxilla.* Mandibles crush the food. Usually the food-handling appendages hold the food for the mandibles to cut into pieces small enough to enter the mouth.

Lobsters have a shortened METAMORPHOSIS with only two types of crustacean larval stages present.   J. C. K.
SEE ALSO: MARINE BIOLOGY, METAMORPHOSIS

Lobworm see Sandworm

Lock see Canal

Lockjaw see Tetanus

Locomotion Locomotion is the power most animals have to move from one place to another. Animals need to move about because their food is organic and usually must be sought out. Some methods of locomotion are walking (man), creeping by action of muscles in the body walls (worm), jumping (grasshopper), swinging (monkey), swimming (fish), and flying (bird).
SEE: ANIMAL

Locomotive see Train, railroad

Locoweed (LOH-koh-weed) Locoweed is one of several plants belonging to the PEA family. It grows in the South and Southwest and when cattle or sheep eat locoweed they develop nervous disorders, becoming "loco." They are unable to control their muscles and may die of starvation.

Blue locoweed

Locus In MATHEMATICS, locus is a line or curve containing all points specified in a problem and no others. In BIOLOGY, locus is the position of a GENE in the lineup of genes on a CHROMOSOME.
SEE: HEREDITY

Locust (insect) see Arthropoda, Grasshopper, Insecta

Locust (tree) (LOH-kuhst) It is a shrub or tree ranging in height from 2 to 100 feet tall. These prickly woody plants have one to three inch thorns on their branches. Many small leaflets make up one leaf. The fruit is a long, brown leathery pod when it is ripe. Flowers may be white, green, pink, or rose in color.

Honey locust is 70 to 80 feet tall with long thorns. Small green flowers appear in spring forming one and one-half-foot flat pods by fall. Black locust, growing about the same height, has small paired thorns. White flowers mature into six-inch fruit. Clammy locust

Locust tree

rarely exceeds 20 feet. It has pink flowers and three-inch pods. Bristly locust ranges between 2 to 10 feet tall. It lacks thorns but has stiff hairs. Its flower is rose colored.

Locust flowers have 5 petals, 5 sepals, 10 stamens and 1 pistil. Pinnately compound LEAVES occur alternately. Margins are smooth or serrated. Some leaflets are also compound. The fruit is a pod or legume. They are members of the family Leguminosae.   H. J. C.
SEE ALSO: LEGUME

Lode A lode is a vein-like deposit of metallic ORE. It occures within definite boundaries which separate it from other nearby ROCK formations.
SEE: MINERALS

Lodestone see Magnetite

Lodgepole pine see Forestry

Loess see Soil types

Loganberry The loganberry is a cross between the BLACKBERRY and the red raspberry. The sharp-tasting berries, which grow on vines, are used fresh, canned or dried. The vine is largely grown on the Pacific coast.

Long ton see Measurements

Loganberry

Longevity Longevity is great age or length of life beyond the usual life expectancy. It depends on one's inherited bodily make-up—usually circulatory and nervous systems—and on environment. Environment includes such things as diet, sanitation, pace of life.
SEE: ANIMALS, LIFE SPAN OF

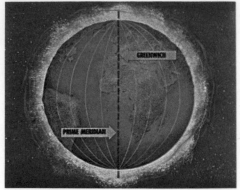
Civil Air Patrol

Lice

Longitude Longitude is the distance east or west measured in degrees or hours of time from a meridian running through Greenwich, England. Meridians are lines of longitude one degree apart which divide EARTH into 360 equal parts. Fifteen degrees equal one hour.

Loon The loon is a large diving bird found in the northern half of the Northern Hemisphere. Like other divers, loons are well protected against the cold of deep water. They are swift swimmers and divers and expert fish and frog catchers. Loons are commonly called the *great northern divers*.

Loons resemble DUCKS but may reach three feet in length. They live in ground nests along a lake edge. The nests are built of sticks, reeds, and moss. A loon usually lays two dark greenish-brown eggs.

Loons are not frequently seen at close range, as they are suspicious and quick to take cover. They are extremely adept at swimming and diving, propelling themselves by means of both feet and wings. The bird has an eery wild cry.   D. J. I.

Lotus see Water lily

Louse The louse is a small insect that attaches itself to another animal and feeds on its host's blood. It is a parasite. Different animals have different kinds of lice. Lice that live on birds or pigs do not move to human beings.

Chewing lice are small, flattened, wingless insects. They have curved claws for clinging to their hosts. Like all insects, they have six legs. They live upon birds and mammals and do not suck blood. They have gradual META-MORPHOSIS because all the young stages look like adults. All stages of metamorphosis are passed through on the host. None of these lice have been known to attack man.

Sucking lice live only on mammals, including man. They are similar in size and shape to chewing lice except they have narrower heads and sucking instead of chewing mouthparts. Some of these carry disease such as *typhus*. These lice have the same type of metamorphosis as the chewing type.

The eggs of lice are called *nits*. They are cemented onto hair or feathers. Human lice may occur in hair on the head, on the body or on the pubic area. Those on the pubis and head are different species. Body lice and head lice are considered to be two varieties of the same species.   J. C. K.
SEE ALSO: INSECTA

Lovebird The lovebird, so named because it always perches close to its mate, is any of various small PARROTS of Africa and South America. It has a short body and tail, with greenish or gray plumage. It makes an excellent caged bird.

Loon

Lovebird

Low-pressure center A low-pressure center is the heart of an area of low pressure called a CYCLONE. Air flowing toward this area of low pressure is caused by the spinning of the earth to whirl around the center and move upward. It whirls in a counterclockwise direction in the Northern Hemisphere. The low pressure center moves eastward across the United States, taking stormy wet WEATHER with it.

SEE: AIR MASSES, WEATHER FORECASTING

Lubrication Lubrication usually has to do with the oiling or greasing of a machine or the moving parts of bicycles and automobiles. Almost any machine or object which moves will move better and with less effort just after it has been lubricated.

The main reason for regular lubrication of the various machines, toys, appliances, and vehicles which are used daily is to reduce friction. Without lubrication friction causes rapid wear on surfaces that move or slide against each other, such as a piston moving in a cylinder, or a shaft turning in a bearing. Friction may also develop heat that starts a fire or causes moving parts to stick together.

There are many lubricants to satisfy nearly every lubricating need. Oils from PETROLEUM are used to lubricate automobiles and other machinery. GRAPHITE, a form of carbon, is used for some bearings. To meet the requirements for some of today's very high temperature and very low temperature operations, lubricants have been developed that are not affected by these extremes. Many of these contain silica compounds. They provide lubrication under all temperature conditions.

H. P. O.

SEE ALSO: FRICTION, MACHINERY

Lumbago see Arthritis

Lumber Lumber is the name used in the United States for timber which has been cut into boards. One of the nation's first industries, lumbering has been one of the most difficult, hazardous, and interesting.

Loading logs to be cut into lumber

Lumberjacks, men of strength and courage, fell the trees. Then, the trees are cut into manageable lengths. This is called *bucking*. Logging is the process of hauling logs to a railroad, river, or highway to be loaded for transportation to the sawmill.

There are two kinds of lumber—hardwood and softwood. HARDWOOD comes from broad-leaved trees and is often beautifully grained; it seldom splinters, but is apt to warp. It is used for making cabinets, paneling, flooring, baseball bats, and other purposes. SOFTWOOD generally comes from cone-bearing trees and is light in weight, stiff, strong, and less apt to warp. Softwood is used for houses, doors, boxes, and millwork.

Some of the important lumber trees are:

Hardwood	Softwood
Walnut	Pine
Hickory	Spruce
Birch	Hemlock
Oak	Fir
Elm	Cedar
Maple	Redwood

Lumber is bought and sold by the *board foot*, which measures one foot long, one foot wide, and one inch thick.

Important by-products of lumber are small objects made for wood trimmings, sawdust, turpentine, pine oil, rosin, rayon, and cellulose from which paper, twine, and phonograph records are made.

J. K. K.

SEE: FOREST PRODUCTS, FORESTRY

Lumen see Candle power

An object which gives off light is luminescent. Such an object may be an organism

Luminescence (loo-mih-NESS-uhns) A substance which can give off LIGHT when it absorbs energy other than heat energy has the property called *luminescence*.

Electroluminescence occurs when electrical energy absorbed by a substance causes the substance to emit light. In devices such as Geissler tubes or electric ARCS, electrons or ions are accelerated to high speed by an electric field. The electrons or ions collide with the molecules of the electroluminescent material and transfer some of their energy to the molecules. The molecules emit this extra energy as light.

Chemiluminescence occurs when energy given off in a chemical reaction excites the molecules of the substance to emit light. When chemiluminescence occurs in living systems, as in the tail of a firefly, it is often called *bioluminescence*.

Photoluminescence or *fluorescence* occurs when light or ionizing radiation absorbed by a substance causes the substance to emit light, as in a fluorescent lamp.

The continued luminescence of a substance for several seconds or minutes after the source of excitation is removed is called *phosphorescence*. A. E. C.

SEE ALSO: PHOSPHORESCENCE, RADIATION

Lunar base (LOO-ner) A lunar base is an establishment on the moon's surface to sustain man and to serve as a center of operations. Man's advance beyond the immediate space surrounding Earth (terrestrial space) will be toward the moon and will proceed in three major steps: (1) a trip around the moon by manned space ships, (2) landing on the moon, and (3) the establishment of one or more lunar bases.

The first step demonstrates man's physiological and technical capability to travel to the moon and back. The second step will demonstrate his capacity to do the still more difficult tasks of descending to the lunar surface, surviving on the moon, and relaunching the space ship on its return flight to Earth from the isolation of this alien world. This will be a tremendous accomplishment, considering the help needed at Cape Kennedy and elsewhere to launch today's missiles. These missiles are smaller than tomorrow's space ships, which a small crew, all alone, must launch from the moon.

Even so, man will not be ready yet to engage in a lunar surface exploration. The MOON, although much smaller than Earth, is nevertheless a gigantic world, compared to man, with vast plains and mountain ranges, craters and hills. Just as a more systematic exploration of the Antarctic could not be undertaken until Admiral Byrd established the famous Little America base, so lunar surface exploration requires a base from which to operate. Actually, the exploration of the moon will take years, and a number of bases will probably be established in time. Therefore, the third step is a necessity and must follow closely the second step.

COMPONENTS OF A LUNAR BASE

Even the simplest lunar base requires the following components: (a) life support sys-

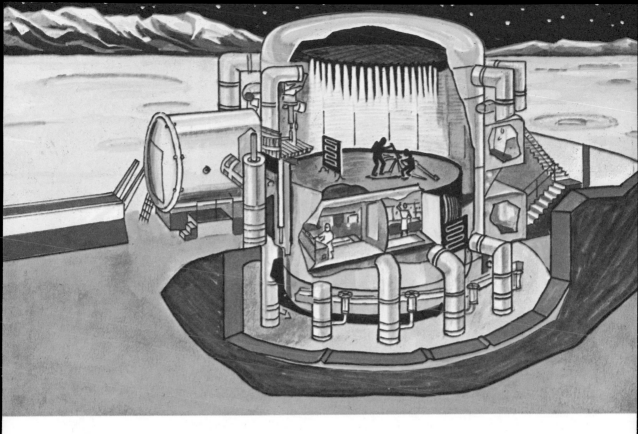

Cross-section of a lunar base (artist's conception). The present plan is to build a lunar base sometime in late 1970s

tem (L.S.S.), (b) power supply system (P.S.S.), and (c) mobile surface system (M.S.S.). The power source of a small base most likely will consist of a NUCLEAR REACTOR. In a heat exchanger, the heat energy of the reactor is transferred from the radioactive reactor coolant fluid to the non-radioactive turbine working fluid. Reactor and heat exchanger are, for safety reasons, widely separated from the L.S.S., which is protected from their dangerous nuclear radiation by the shielding effect of many feet of lunar rock.

The *power generation system,* to which the crew must have ready access for maintenance and repair, is next to the L.S.S. proper, to which it delivers its electric power. The L.S.S. consists of four major sections which do not necessarily have to be rigidly separated. The *control section* contains the entire data handling system, supervising the operation of all stationary base equipment. It maintains contact with, and monitors, all outside operations including the moon-mobiles, and it maintains contact with the earth and supervises all space ship landings and take-offs as well as the dropping of supplies from nonlanding space ships.

The *ecological section* consists of food and oxygen supply systems, waste control and utilization systems, living and recreation space. Such play areas eventually may include a gym, entertainment, film library, book film library (conventional books would be too heavy and bulky), a television theater for direct program reception from Earth, and a swimming pool.

The *laboratory section* contains equipment and instruments for lunar research to evaluate electric, magnetic, temperature, and radiation measurements made by the moon-mobiles on their trips or by using fixed measuring stations which send data back to the base. The researchers would analyze soil specimens gathered at various distances from the base and at various depths. *Seismographs* would be used to detect possible natural moonquakes or to analyze artificial moonquakes caused by explosive missiles impacting at various distances from the base. Biological equipment would be needed to search for traces of life.

The *maintenance section* is equipped with the proper spare parts and tools to carry out all necessary repairs and to keep the entire little outpost operating safely and smoothly. The L.S.S. has a number of exits (more than one for safety) for individuals or for moon-mobiles which can be locked tightly, thus enabling the crew to enter the

Vehicles, such as the proposed moon-mobiles above, will be built to help support life

base directly from the mobile without donning a space suit. This not only is more convenient for loading and unloading cargo, but the arrangement is also more rapid in case of an emergency.

The airlocks serving the moon-mobiles are part of the M.S.S. whose most important items are, of course, the moon-mobiles. The moon-mobiles are the fleet which most likely will consist of automatic instrument-laden vehicles, remote-controlled from the base or outlying posts on elevated places, and of manned vehicles, enabling base crews to carry out more extended scouting trips than would be possible if they had to carry all equipment (including the vital oxygen, water, and food supply) themselves. The various methods of locomotion of the moon-mobile raises further problems.

LOCATION OF A LUNAR BASE

Where on the moon should such a base be established? The first base should be on the side of the moon closest to Earth in order to allow ready radio contact with Earth. However, since the lunar backside, which is forever turned away from earth, is even less known than the visible side, the base should perhaps not be too far away from it; that is, it should be somewhat on the edge of the lunar disc as seen from the earth. Seen from the base, Earth would then stand near the moon's horizon.

Where on the lunar periphery should it be located? The lunar poles appear more attractive than the east or west limb for two reasons. First, the day and night cycle is more moderate, especially because the day temperatures do not rise as high as in more southerly latitudes, since the sun does not rise so high above the horizon. This has a moderating effect even in the absence of an ATMOSPHERE. Second, near the poles there

are crater holes and hills into which the sun never shines. Being in the eternal night, their surface is extremely cold. If large meteors, originating from comets which consist largely of ice (mainly water and ammonia ice) ever fell into these areas, the ice would stay for hundreds or thousands of years without melting or evaporating appreciably. Finding a supply of surface ice on the moon is at least as vital as finding an oasis in the middle of a gigantic desert, because it would make the base partly self-sufficient and would greatly reduce the cost of base supply from the earth. Although the existence of ice is not yet proven, it stands to reason that the first bases will be established near such deposits, should they exist. The strategic significance of ice deposits is great; for, although a nation cannot, with one base, deny another power access to the moon, she could very well claim and control ice deposits and thereby place the other power at a distinct disadvantage of either having to depend on permission to use some of the deposits or having to carry water and oxygen supply from Earth and to continue to do so as the base grows. Whether or not a natural ice deposit exists, it appears that the polar regions are especially attractive as initial base locations for exploration parties.

BUILDING A LUNAR BASE

How would a base be built? To gain protection from small meteorites which hit the airless moon with full force and from dangerous cosmic rays and solar flare radiation, the base (at least most of the L.S.S.) should be underground. Tunnels might be bored by carrying equipment to the moon and drilling into mountain flanks; for example, one tunnel for the L.S.S. and one for the nuclear reactor, separating them by several hundred feet of rock. Or the bottom of sufficiently wide but not too deep lunar rills could be used, covering up part of the rill containing the L.S.S. with a flat roof structure on which soil and rock is piled. In any case, it appears that some soil-moving equipment will have to be carried to the moon, since most of the base is preferably located underground.

Could a lunar base ever become self-sufficient (independent of supply from earth) as far as its basic necessities are concerned? At this time scientists cannot be absolutely certain; but the answer to this question is most likely to be "Yes." There is every reason to assume that lunar soil and rocks consist of compounds which contain the elements silicon, nitrogen, oxygen, hydrogen, and some carbon, as on the earth. With unlimited nuclear power available, the vital elements oxygen and hydrogen as well as nitrogen can be extracted from the lunar rocks. Oxygen and nitrogen would be used to form the base atmosphere. Oxygen and hydrogen could form water. Nitrogen could be used together with other elements to manufacture artificial fertilizers to amend natural human waste fertilizer for algae cultures, as well as for plant farming. The ALGAE would be used for oxygen supply as well as for food. Thus, it must be expected that lunar bases eventually will be capable of operating without help from Earth as long as their nuclear power lasts, or indefinitely, if they can be operated entirely on solar power. The ideal location for solar-powered bases is at the poles, where, at some elevation, solar radiation is permanently available to be collected in large reflectors, heating a working fluid which in turn drives a turbo-generator system.

Lunar bases will represent man's first extraterrestrial establishments with a significant degree of independence. They will be of vital importance for lunar and solar research, as well as for stellar research using very large optical telescopes, which benefit from the absence of an atmosphere, and gigantic radio-telescopes, which utilize the shape of suitable craters as natural antenna configurations. Finally, lunar bases will be, in many respects, man's springboard to the planets of our solar system.   K. A. E.

SEE ALSO: ASTRONAUTICS, COSMONAUT, SPACE, SPACE MEDICINE, SPACE TRAVEL, SPACE VEHICLES

Lunar eclipse see Eclipse

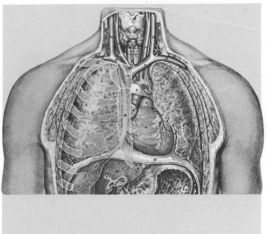

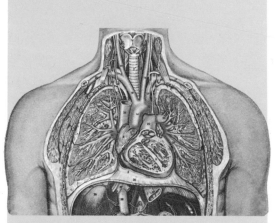

©Denoyer-Geppert Co.

Interior (bottom) and exterior (top) views of the lungs, location and inside parts

Lung The lungs are organs of breathing. Most animals that live on land have lungs. They bring the oxygen of the air to the blood and take away carbon dioxide from the blood.

There are two lungs, one on each side of the chest. The right lung is larger and has three lobes: upper, middle, and lower. The left lung is slightly smaller and has only upper and lower lobes.

The lungs fit snugly into the cavity of the chest. They are protected by the ribs and by a thin covering called the *pleura*. The DIAPHRAGM, a powerful muscle, separates the lungs from the abdominal space. The diaphragm pushes air out of the lungs and then relaxes to allow the lungs to fill with air. This is one way that breathing takes place.

The heart lies between the lungs in the chest cavity and sends large blood vessels into the lungs. These vessels divide into smaller and smaller vessels that circulate a large amount of blood through the lungs.

The air enters the lungs from the nose or mouth through a large windpipe called the *trachea*. The trachea branches into smaller pipes that go to each lung, the right and left *bronchi*. Each bronchus branches like a tree into smaller *bronchioles* which end in many small sacs called *alveoli*. This network of air passages and blood vessels gives the lung its spongy red appearance.

Because oxygen is necessary for the body cells to live, fresh oxygen must constantly be provided when the cells use up their supply. CARBON DIOXIDE is a waste gas that must be removed so that it does not poison the cells. The tiny alveoli have surfaces that are moist and thin, and they are surrounded by small blood vessels. It is here that an exchange of gases takes place. When air is inhaled, these tiny sacs blow up like balloons. The blood picks up the oxygen and transports it to all the cells of the body. Carbon dioxide passes from the blood into the alveoli and is expelled when these little balloons deflate.

A healthy lung has ten times the number of alveoli that are necessary to life. A normal person takes about eighteen to twenty breaths a minute. Each breath contains about a pint of air. After hard exercise, a person might take in as much as 125 quarts of air a minute. The walls of the bronchial tree are lined with epithelium and contain a layer of smooth muscle which widens or narrows the bronchial tubes to meet the body's demands.

If a person has had some lung damage, he may be able to take only up to fifty quarts of air a minute. This means that he is capable of only a limited amount of exertion before being out of breath.

The air that is breathed into the body must be warmed to the body temperature of 98.6° F. The body becomes cooler as it loses some of its heat to the air. Animals often pant in an effort to cool off.

TUBERCULOSIS, PNEUMONIA, and BRONCHITIS are diseases of the lung caused by bacteria. PLEURISY is an infection of the covering (pleura) of the lungs. Many allergies affect the tissues of the lungs, causing the breathlessness of asthma.   B. J. C.

SEE ALSO: CIRCULATORY SYSTEM, GILLS, RESPIRATORY SYSTEM, TRACHEA

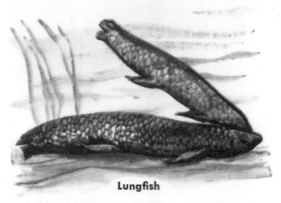

Lungfish

Lungfish The lungfish has both gills and lungs (*swimbladder*) for breathing. In dry seasons, it is able to form a cocoon around itself and hibernate in the mud.

Millions of years ago lungfish were abundant, but there are now only three known kinds. The Australian lungfish (*Neoceratodus forsteri*) is the largest. They are found only in the Burnett and Mary Rivers of Queensland. They use their lungs to aid in breathing, but they do not form cocoons.

Two similar genera, one of South America and one of Central America, have slender bodies, small scales, and long, paired fins. They live in seasonal swamps, breathing with their gills in the wet season. During the dry season, they form mucus-lined cocoons and estivate. At this time, respiration is entirely by means of the lungs.   I. H. S.

Lunisolar precession Lunisolar precession is the apparent change in the location of the stars in relation to the observers on Earth. It is caused by the pull of *gravity* of the sun and the moon on the earth.

Lunisolar precession

NORTH

PULL OF MOON'S GRAVITY

PULL OF SUN'S GRAVITY

AMOUNT OF PRECESSION

Actually, the earth's axis is almost fixed at an angle of 23½ degrees to the plane of its equator. But the gravitational effect of the sun and moon (sometimes supplementing, sometimes counteracting each other) causes the axis of the spinning Earth to wobble slightly, as in the motion of a spinning top. The result is that the stars used as reference points (such as the North star or the constellations) seem to move slowly westward, completing a cycle in about 26,000 years.   C. L. K.

SEE ALSO: EARTH, EQUINOX

U.S. Department of Agriculture photo

Blue lupine, used in crop rotation

Lupine It is a flowering herb which grows about three feet tall. Seven to nine slender leaflets make up one single leaf. They are arranged on the petiole like fingers extending from your palm. Flowers may be yellow, blue, white, or rose in color.

Lupine is an annual or perennial plant. The latter variety possesses a taproot which stores starch for the next spring's growth. Each FLOWER on the inflorescence has 5 petals, 5 sepals, 10 stamens and 1 pistil. The ovary matures into a pod fruit.

A few shrubs about 6 feet high are also called lupine. They all belong to family Leguminosae. Annual lupine is used to improve soil fertility, a characteristic typical of other members of legumes.   H. J. C.

SEE ALSO: GRASSES

Lutetium (loo-TEE-shuhm) Lutetium, element number 71, is the last metal in the lanthanide series of RARE-EARTH elements. It is like LANTHANUM and the other lanthanides in that its compounds are colorless and not magnetic. Lutetium was named after the Roman name of Paris, France.

The lanthanide elements have properties remarkably alike. The similarity occurs because each element has two electrons in the outermost shell. Because of the great similarity in chemical properties, it is difficult to isolate one rare earth like lutetium from the others.

Lutetium (symbol Lu) was first separated from YTTERBIUM in 1907. It has an atomic weight of 174.97 (174.99, O=16). It is sometimes spelled *lutecium*.   J. R. S.

SEE ALSO: ATOM, ELEMENTS

Lux Lux is the amount of illumination received on a surface one meter from a light source which is considered as one unit. The lux is an international unit which equals 0.0929 candela.

SEE: CANDLE POWER, LIGHT

Lye Lye is a term used for a type of very strong alkali. Its chemical name is *sodium hydroxide*. Lye as a chemical has many uses. Its white powder destroys waste by its ability to eat organic material. It is used in the making of hard soap and textiles, in tanning LEATHER, in refining petroleum, and in the canning industry.

Lye is soluble in water and is a good CONDUCTOR of electricity. It neutralizes acids and can turn litmus paper blue. It can dissolve wool but not cotton.

Lye is very injurious to skin, and actual contact with it must be avoided because of its caustic, or burning, nature.

The chemical formula for lye is NaOH. Lye is manufactured from calcium hydroxide and sodium carbonate reacting to form sodium hydroxide (lye) and calcium carbonate.   D. E. Z.

SEE ALSO: ACIDS AND BASES

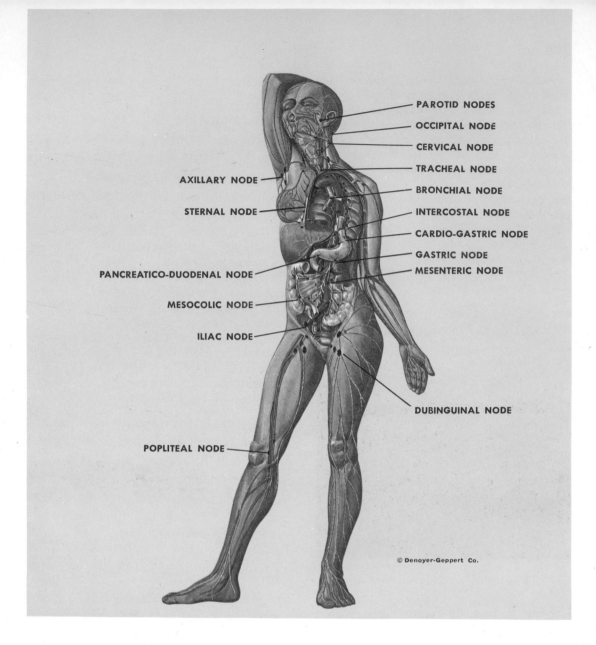

PAROTID NODES

OCCIPITAL NODE

CERVICAL NODE

TRACHEAL NODE

BRONCHIAL NODE

AXILLARY NODE

INTERCOSTAL NODE

STERNAL NODE

CARDIO-GASTRIC NODE

GASTRIC NODE

MESENTERIC NODE

PANCREATICO-DUODENAL NODE

MESOCOLIC NODE

ILIAC NODE

DUBINGUINAL NODE

POPLITEAL NODE

© Denoyer-Geppert Co.

Lymphatic system (limm-FAT-ick) In the bodies of vertebrate animals there is a system of special vessels and glands called the *lymphatic system.* Blood cells that fight disease, as well as special body fluids, move through this system. The system serves the important tasks of purifying blood, helping to fight INFECTION, and storing and moving the vital white cells and tissue fluids. There are many lymph glands in the human body. The paired TONSILS in the throat and the ADENOIDS in the nose are two of them.

The lymph vessels are both alike and different from the blood vessels. Like the veins, lymph vessels help return body fluids to the heart. Unlike veins, they contain no red blood cells. Like the veins, they do not receive the direct pumping force of the heart. The heart acts directly to push blood only through the arteries.

THE COURSE OF LYMPH CIRCULATION

Blood capillaries connect at one end with arteries and at the other with veins. Unlike this, the tiny lymph capillaries start as dead-end finger-like tubes. Then millions of these lymph vessels come together to form larger vessels (*lymphatic ducts*). All along their course, they collect colorless fluid called lymph, and white cells that have previously moved out through the capillary walls. The lymphatic ducts have pocket-like flaps or valves (as do larger veins) to prevent backflow of the lymph.

In hundreds of places along the lymph vessels, there are networks of tissues called *nodes* or *lymph glands*. These lymph glands serve mainly to store extra fluid and cells and to manufacture, by cell division, many new white cells (lymphocytes).

When a person is sick with a cold or other infection, he may notice certain sore swellings in his neck, or his tonsils may be tender and enlarged. Such swelling is evidence of the battle going on between mobilized white cells and the invading germs.

The lymphatic system does not end in the lymph glands. If it did, body and blood liquids would gather there, causing swelling and robbing the blood of its lost cells and fluids. Instead, additional lymph ducts lead out of each gland. Still other lymph vessels come from the intestinal walls laden with soluble fats from the ingested foods. These vessels join others, forming into two still larger (one-quarter inch diameter) vessels. These are called *thoracic ducts*. They are located in the upper chest, under the collar bone. They join directly into the main upper red-blood vein and thus return many white cells and most of the highly-traveled body fluids back to the heart for redistribution through the arterial system.

THE CONTENTS OF THE LYMPH

The lymph fluid contains living white cells and a complex watery substance. The white cells are of several kinds. Ordinary leucocytes are ameba-like cells which are also present in the red blood. They can form finger-like extensions which they wrap about any germs or even dust particles in the lymph or the fluid between other body cells. Such engulfing action is called *phagocytic action*. The bacteria and other foreign bodies are really eaten and then destroyed by the white cells. The lymph nodes or glands can manufacture some white cells of a similar but distinct type. These *phagocytes* are called *lymphocytes*. Finally, the non-cellular fluid of the lymph is composed of water, dissolved minerals, foods, oxygen enroute from the blood to cells, and carbon dioxide and other cell wastes. In summary, lymph is like the red blood except that it contains no red cells and, unlike blood plasma, it has none of the heavier blood proteins whose molecules are too large to push through the capillary walls. Lymph is unique because it has oxygen only in solution and it carries some fatty fluids, wastes, and many white cells not found in the red blood.

The lymph glands have special values not served by other body organs. Each node is a network of fibers which forms a fine screen for bacteria. In these fibers are millions of white cells which eat up the enmeshed bacteria. When some region of the body far away is infected with germs, the white cells move out into the red-blood stream (by the thoracic duct) and gather to attack the distant invader.

The fact that the lymph vessels lack a pumping organ leads to an important health lesson. How does lymph keep up a healthy circulation of its needed cells and fluid? The answer is that it does it only as a result of vigorous physical exercise and deep breathing. Only by the massaging activity of the muscular organs surrounding the lymph vessels and glands can healthy circulation of this life fluid be maintained.   L. M.

SEE ALSO: BLOOD, CIRCULATORY SYSTEM

Lynx see Cat family

Lyrebird The lyrebird is an Australian song bird. It is about the size of a hen and has a rather plain brownish body. The tail of the male is brightly plumed, however, and when fully developed resembles an ancient lyre. Although a poor flyer, the bird can run very fast. It is a good mimic.

Lyrebird

Macadam (muh-KADD-um) Macadam is the name of a popular road surface. It was introduced in England in the early nineteenth century by John Loudon McAdam, a Scotsman. The need for economical as well as durable road paving has always existed. McAdam's contribution in this field made him one of the leading figures in the history of road-making.

His technique was basically simple. The roadbed was covered with layers of crushed rocks of about two inches on a side. Moving coaches and wagons packed them, the many rocks adjusting themselves to each other to give a stable, solid road.

Variations on the basic plan utilize clay, tar, or other tar-like substances as fillers and binding agents. Today any road built of gravel or crushed rock and bound by tar or asphalt is referred to as a macadam road. Sometimes an over-layer of ASPHALT mixtures is used to give a yet smoother surface, known as *black top*.   D. J. I.

Macaw (muh-KAW) Macaws are brightly-colored, long-tailed tropical birds found in the jungles of tropical and subtropical America. They belong to the PARROT family and have the brilliant red, blue, yellow, and green feathers, loud screaming voices, and large arched bills typical of that group of birds.

Macaws, who usually live in pairs, have long lives. Some have been known to live over one hundred years. They are temperamental birds with unusual abilities. When captured young, they may be taught to imitate words and obey commands. However, when captured as adult birds, macaws are often vicious and not easily trained. In the jungle, macaws eat palm fruit, seeds, and nuts which they crack with their large and powerful beaks. In captivity they are fed oats, canary seed, corn, crackers, sliced carrots, turnips, and tomatoes. One of the most beautiful macaws is the red and blue macaw, which is brilliantly colored in scarlet red, pale blue, and chrome yellow.   D. J. A.

Mace Mace is the outer coat of a seed that grows on a tropical tree. It is bright red when it is opened but turns a light brownish-tan after drying. Mace is a valued spice. It is also used in many medicines. The seed itself is known as *nutmeg*.

Mace grows on *Myristica fragrans,* a deciduous tree found wild in the Molucca Islands and New Guinea. It has been planted in many localities of the tropics but thrives best in its native area. Nearly the whole surface of the Molucca Islands is covered with these trees. The tree is medium-sized with handsome, dark evergreen leaves, oval and pointed in shape.   M. R. L.

SEE ALSO: NUTMEG

Mace plant and seed coat

Mach, Ernst (MOCK) (1838-1916) Ernst Mach was an Austrian physicist and philosopher whose ideas about research and physical science made it possible for ALBERT EINSTEIN to work out his theory of relativity. Mach's studies of bodies moving through gases at high speeds gave rise to the use of the term *Mach Number. Mach 1,* for example, is the speed of sound.

Mach 0.5 is half the speed of sound. *Mach 2* is twice the speed of sound.

Although the results of Ernst Mach's experiments were published, they were not noticed or used until airplanes began to approach speeds close to the speed of sound. His work has had great influence on modern scientific thought.

Born at Turos, Moravia, February 18, 1838, Mach was educated in Vienna. He served as professor of physics at the University of Graz from 1864-1867, at the University of Prague from 1867-1895, and as professor of philosophy at the University of Vienna from 1895-1901. In 1901 he was elevated to the Austrian peerage. He died near Munich, Germany, February 19, 1916.

D. H. J.

Machinery Machinery consists of complex machines. Such complex machines may be defined as *two or more simple machines connected together*. There are six simple machines: the lever, the wheel and axle, the pulley, the inclined plane, the wedge, and the screw. These simple machines are all used to help men do different kinds of work—to lift, carry, turn, pull, and cut. A combination of any of the simple machines is a complex machine. Most complex machines are designed to do special kinds of work.

One of the complex machines easiest to understand is the gear. A *gear* is made up of two simple wheel and axle machines placed next to one another. When one turns, it causes the other to turn. Usually the wheels are of different sizes and have teeth cut into their edges to prevent slipping. The smaller gear turns faster, with less turning force, than the larger gear, which then has more turning force. Every time the small gear turns all the way around, the large gear turns only part way. The large wheel and its axle are turning more slowly

but can lift something heavier or turn something too difficult for the axle of the small wheel. By cutting the edge of the gears at an angle, the axes of rotation of the two gears can be at an angle with each other rather than being along the same direction. In this way, a force in a vertical direction can

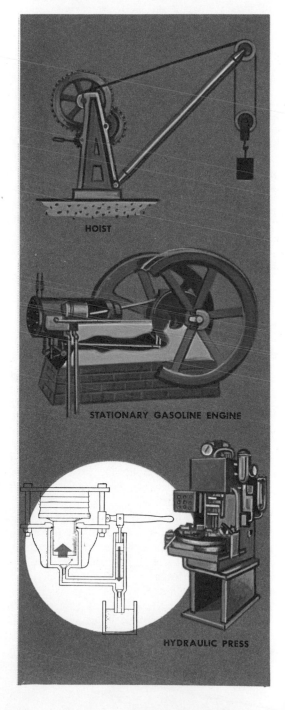

HOIST

STATIONARY GASOLINE ENGINE

HYDRAULIC PRESS

be changed to one in a horizontal direction. Gears are used in watches, automobiles, outboard motors, trains, and many other complex machines.

ENERGY AND PURPOSES OF COMPLEX MACHINES

In order to do work that muscles are not strong enough to do, the strength of forces in nature have been used. In earlier times, the force of wind, of moving water, of combustion, of steam, and, more recently, chemical, electrical, magnetic, atomic, and nuclear forces—all have been harnessed to mechanical motions, based on the six simple machines. Combinations of these simple machines have been devised that can perform a large variety of mechanical motions. By linking together these motions with each other, complex machinery for many specialized purposes has been developed.

The purpose of complex machinery is to do work by transforming motion and ENERGY. The work to be done can vary from pulling out a nail, moving a vehicle—airplane, automobile, ship, train—and taking a picture, to solving mathematical problems. In a machine, the mechanical energy required to do the job is transferred by mechanical parts (variations of the six basic machines). Many machines also transform one form of energy into another form. For example: heat energy from burning coal may be used to make steam from water. The steam may be used in a steam engine to produce mechanical energy. Such energy may be used to run a DYNAMO to generate electricity. The electrical energy from the dynamo may in turn be converted into heat energy (electric stove, iron), mechanical energy (electric motor), light energy (electric light), sound energy (loudspeaker), radiant energy (X-ray machine), and so forth.

Not only do machines transfer and transform energy, but they can multiply force or effort. Thus certain machines enable a feeble force operating through a certain distance to move a larger force through a smaller distance. This increase in effort occurs in a system of pulleys, such as a block and tackle, or a gear assembly found in an automobile transmission. Other machines can multiply speed by increasing effort, as in a BICYCLE. A machine cannot gain force and speed at the same time.

HISTORICAL DEVELOPMENT

The history of machines parallels the search for forces to help man's muscles. Wind and running water, from which water wheels and windmills were developed, were probably among the first complex machines used by man. The wind or running water forces the big blades of a windmill or water wheel to turn (wheel and axle); by bending the axle and attaching a lever, the rotary motion becomes an up and down motion, which can make a pump handle go up and down; or by adding gears to the turning axle, the force or speed can be increased and used to grind grain, drive looms, sharpen knives.

There is not always enough wind, and running water is not available everywhere. A more universal source of power is steam, but was not put to use until the 1700's, when a steam pump was developed to pump water out of the coal mines in England. This led to the invention of the steam engine. The principle is simple: a fire heats water and turns it into steam which, if confined in a cylinder with a movable piston, has the power to push the piston. The movement of the piston can be transferred to the wheels of a train or the water wheel of a boat.

Gasoline and diesel ENGINES were developed next—in the early 1900's. The power to run them came from fire, a fire that burns so fast that it is called an *explosion*. If the explosion—of gasoline mixed with air—takes place in a cylinder into which a piston is fitted, the explosion will push the piston and its rod. If several successive explosions take place in several cylinders, and all the pistons are connected to the same shaft or axle, up and down movements will be transformed to rotary movement.

During the 1800's electrical power was discovered. By turning a coil of wire between the poles of a MAGNET, an electric current could be made to flow in the wire. If the wire through which electricity is flowing were wound into a coil, this coil acted as a magnet and could attract iron or steel. From these discoveries came the electric generator, or dynamo, for producing large amounts of electric power cheaply, and the electric motor. Electric power could be transmitted easily through wires to machines in homes and factories, where it could be transformed by motors into mechanical power.

WINDMILL

WATER WHEEL

ELECTRIC MOTOR

SOLAR BATTERY

GASOLINE ENGINE

JET ENGINE

Large, electrically-driven machine tools were built—machines which could make metal parts for other machines, lathes that could hold and cut perfectly round pieces of steel, planers that could slice pieces of metal any thickness, drills and milling machines for making holes and grooves, hydraulic presses to form sheet metal into desired shapes. These machines, run by electric power, were designed to turn out identical, precise mechanical parts. Parts, screws, gears, cams, rachets, link chains, belt drives, roller bearings were interchangeable from machine to machine and made mass production possible.

The search for new sources of power continues and new mechanisms must be developed for these. Jet engines, rocket engines, nuclear reactors, fuel cells, solar batteries, ionic engines, thermoelectric generators, and nuclear batteries are some of the new power sources now being developed. New materials with special properties are often needed with these new power sources; for example, special metal alloys and ceramics to withstand very high temperatures, materials of very high purity, and so forth.

All modern machines combine mechanical principles of force and motion with the special properties of matter and energy. As more is understood about matter and energy, suitable machinery will be devised. For example, hydraulic pumps and automatic transmission systems were developed after the effects of pressure on air and water were investigated; the ball point pen was developed after molecular adhesion was understood. H. W. M.

SEE ALSO: AUTOMATION; AUTOMOBILE; ELECTRONICS; ENGINE; FORCES; HYDRAULIC ACTION; MACHINES, SIMPLE; POWER; PRESSURE; PUMP; SPEED; WINDMILL; WORK

✳ THINGS TO DO

HOW MUCH FORCE DO YOU EXERT GOING UP TO SECOND FLOOR?

1 The length of an inclined plane divided by the height gives you the mechanical advantage. The weight of the body divided by the mechanical advantage is equal to the pounds of force needed to reach the top of the ramp.

2 Compare this with the amount of force when you climb the same height straight up a ladder.

3 Study the illustrations above. Then use your own weight and an inclined plane to determine how much force is exerted and how much work was accomplished.

Machines, simple The use of machines has enabled man to do work that he lacks the power to do unaided. Machines have also made it possible for him to harness the forces in the wind, in fuels, and in water. Without machines man would still exist in a primitive state and the progress he has made could never have come about.

A machine is any device used to increase force, change the direction of force, or increase speed in performing WORK. Work is done only if something is moved by overcoming a resistance, such as friction or gravity. A simple machine has no energy source within it, so it cannot do work unless work is put into it.

Where FRICTION causes only negligible loss of energy, work produced by a machine equals the amount of work put into it. This work of machines is measurable. It is the *product of the unit of force and distance.* For example, if a person lifts a ten pound box three feet, he has done three times ten pounds or thirty foot-pounds of work.

The MECHANICAL ADVANTAGE of a machine is the ratio of resistance to effort. For example, a man lifts fifty pounds of weight by applying ten pounds of effort to a lever. Then the mechanical advantage of the lever is five to one.

There are machines of all kinds and sizes in existence today, but no matter how complex they may appear, all machines are a combination of several simple machines or modifications of one. A simple machine is one that is moved by just one force. There are six such machines: the lever, wheel and axle, pulley, inclined plane, screw, and wedge.

The *lever* is a long plank, beam, or bar that is used to move heavy loads. ARCHIMEDES, a Greek mathematician, discovered the law of the lever and stated that if he were given a long enough stick and a place to stand, he could move the world. The beam rests on a firm object called the *fulcrum.* The *point of resistance* is the place where the load to be moved is located. The point where the force is applied to move the load is the *point of effort.* The closer the fulcrum is to the load, the less effort it takes to move the load.

There are three classes of levers with the fulcrum, force, and load in different positions. In *first-class levers,* the fulcrum is located between the force and the load. Some first-class levers are seesaws, crowbars, and scissors. Levers of the *second class* always have the load between the force and the fulcrum. Examples of this kind of lever are the wheelbarrow and the nutcracker. In *third-class levers,* the force is between the resistance (load) and the fulcrum. These levers do not increase force but make it possible for objects to be moved greater distances more quickly. Examples of the third-class levers are the broom, tweezers, and ice-tongs.

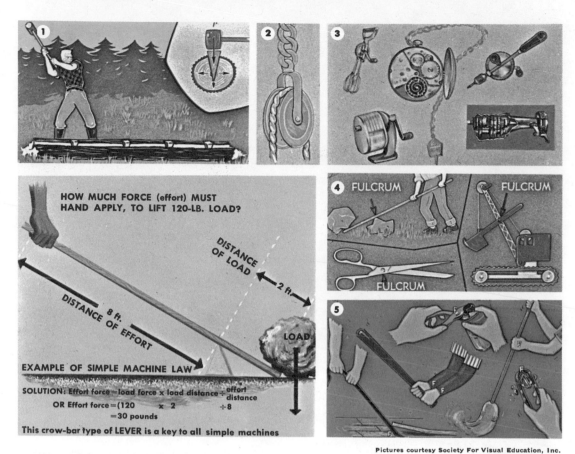

In the illustration:

1 HOW MUCH FORCE (effort) MUST HAND APPLY, TO LIFT 120-LB. LOAD?

DISTANCE OF LOAD — 2 ft.

DISTANCE OF EFFORT — 8 ft.

LOAD

EXAMPLE OF SIMPLE MACHINE LAW

SOLUTION: Effort force = load force × load distance ÷ effort distance

OR Effort force = (120 × 2 ÷ 8

= 30 pounds

This crow-bar type of LEVER is a key to all simple machines

4 FULCRUM FULCRUM FULCRUM

(1) The wedge can help split a log. (2) A fixed pulley changes direction of a force. (3) Many familiar objects include wheel and axle. (4) A lever must be placed on a fulcrum to do work. (5) Hands can serve as a fulcrum

A *wheel* is a cylindrical object that rotates about the axis of the cylinder. The axle is a rigid rod that goes through the center of the wheel and lies along the cylinder axis. The wheel and axle are dealt with as a single unit when they are rigidly joined to each other and work together as a unit.

There are different kinds of wheels for different kinds of work. The wheels on cars, and trains, are familiar examples. They enable man to move about speedily over great distances. Wheels also make it possible to move heavy objects more easily. If someone were to try to pull a box of sand down the street, there would be so much friction or rubbing between the box and the ground that the box would be difficult to move. But, put wheels on the box and it will move more easily because less friction is produced.

Some wheels turn other wheels, like the geared wheels on a bicycle or those on an egg beater or those in clocks and watches. Some wheels turn axles so that both turn together. Common examples are doorknobs, knobs on the radio and television, and the knob that controls the steam in a radiator.

A *pulley* is a *grooved wheel*. A rope is fitted into the groove and turns the wheel when pulled. A *fixed* pulley is attached to a support, and when one end of the rope is fastened to a load the load moves up. Force is not increased, but its direction has been changed. The person can stay in one place and use the weight of his body to help lift the load instead of carrying it.

A *block and tackle* consists of a fixed pulley, a movable pulley to which the load is attached, and several strands of rope. A block and tackle is used to increase mechanical advantage. The mechanical advantage increases with the number of strands of rope attached to the movable pulley. Increasing the number of strands means that the applied force must act over a longer distance.

The *inclined plane* is a very simple machine. It is a sloping surface that makes it easier to pull, push, or roll heavy loads. Instead of lifting a piano onto a truck, the movers can put a sturdy plank from the ground to the truck and roll the piano up onto the truck. They will use less effort but this effort has to be exerted over the greater

DOES A FIXED OR MOVABLE PULLEY MAKE WORK EASIER?

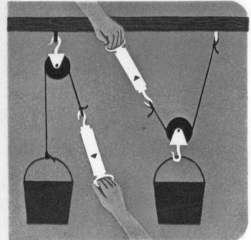

1 Construct a support on which to fasten a stationary or fixed pulley. Thread heavy cord through the pulley.
2 Weigh a pail of water and record the weight. Tie one end of the cord to the handle of the pail. Tie the other end to a spring scale.
3 Now measure the force needed to raise the pail with a fixed pulley.
4 By following the diagrams set up a movable pulley on the support. Repeat the experiment.
5 Did it take much less effort than with a fixed pulley? It should cut your force about in half if the pulleys are well lubricated.

HOW CAN YOU MAKE A WHEEL AND AXLE DO MORE WORK FOR YOU?

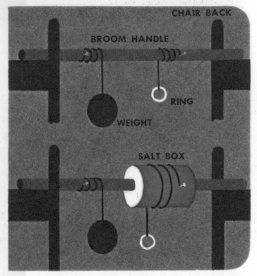

1 Construct a windlass by following the accompanying diagram.
2 Weigh a heavy object with a spring scale. Record the figure.
3 Now tie the object to the cord which is fastened to the axle of the windlass. Turn the wheel arm by pulling with a spring scale.
4 Now insert a longer wheel arm into the end of the axle. Pull the load now with the spring scale.
5 Does the size of the wheel affect the amount of work necessary to lift an object?

distance the load now travels. A stairway is an inclined plane with steps forming its slope. In some places, such as baseball parks, people move from one level to another by way of ramps, which are inclined planes.

The *screw* is an inclined plane wound at its edge on a cylinder or cone. Archimedes is given credit for inventing the screw. A screw develops very large forces for lifting heavy weights and producing great pressures. Consider how tightly the threads hold two pieces of wood together or how a set of jackscrews can lift a house off the ground, how a jack lifts a car, and how tightly a vise holds metal and wood for cutting or shaping. The practical applications of the screw in common household fixtures are nu-

merous: faucets, screw-in bulbs, screw-on bottle tops, any connection of water pipes, etc.

The *wedge* is essentially an inclined plane. The longer a wedge is compared to its thickness, the easier it is to force it through things. People who split logs use a wedge which is struck with an axe and driven into the wood. The farther it goes, the farther apart the two sections of the log move. Wedges increase force and are the basis of all cutting and piercing tools such as knives, needles, chisels, axes, nails, tacks, and pins, all of which push apart paper, wood, or cloth as they are driven in by pounding or pushing.

D. C. H.

SEE ALSO: ENERGY, MACHINERY, WORK

Mackerel

Mackerel These are saltwater fish with almost scaleless skins. Their tails are deeply forked and narrow sharply where they join the body. Behind both the dorsal (along the back) and anal (bottom or ventral side nearest the tail end) are a number of tiny finlets.

Their skins are silvery and iridescent. Their bodies are slender and streamlined. Patterns vary with the species but are usually confined to the dorsal side.

Mackerel swim swiftly and travel in schools that cover large areas. They live both off-shore and far out at sea. Many species have commercial value. Mackerel, along with bonito and TUNA, belong in the family *Scombridae*. It has worldwide distribution. J. C. K.

Madder Madder is a plant that has prickly leaves, small yellowish flowers and a fruit of black berries. The long fleshy roots have been used for thousands of years to produce beautiful colors, especially purple and orange. Cloth colored by madder DYES has been found in Egyptian mummy cases.

Madonna lily see Lily

Maelstrom see Whirlpool

Maggot see Fly, Larva

Madder

Magnesia (magg-NEE-zhuh) Magnesia, or magnesium oxide, is a white, powdery chemical without odor or taste. When mixed with water, it becomes *milk of magnesia* which is used as a laxative and an antacid for digestive ailments and acid poisoning.

Because of its high melting point and its low heat conductivity, it is used in insulation covering for furnaces and hot pipes. It is commonly made by heating the mineral magnesite, by electrochemical treatment of magnesium salts from sea water, or by burning magnesium metal in air. D. A. B.

Magnesium (magg-NEE-zhuhm) Magnesium is a light and shiny metal element. It is chemically active and when heated burns with a blinding and brilliant white light. SIR HUMPHRY DAVY first prepared elementary magnesium in 1807.

Flash bulbs contain magnesium wire and oxygen. When the camera shutter is snapped, a small electric current from a battery ignites the wire and produces the flash. Incendiary BOMBS and flares also contain magnesium.

Since magnesium is a light metal (density 1.74), it is used where lightness is important, as in airplanes. Magnesium compounds include asbestos, talc and Epsom salts.

Magnesium (symbol Mg) is element number 12 and its atomic weight is 24.312 (24.32, O$=$16). J. R. S.
SEE ALSO: ATOM, ELEMENTS

Magnet A magnet is a body which has the property of attracting certain metals such as iron and steel. If a magnet is suspended on a string or fine wire, it will turn until it aligns itself in a north-south direction.

Mankind has known about magnetism for centuries. There is evidence that the first natural magnets were found in a place in Asia Minor called *Magnesia*. These natural magnets consist of an oxide of iron called *magnetite*. When this ore is found in the magnetized state, it is given the

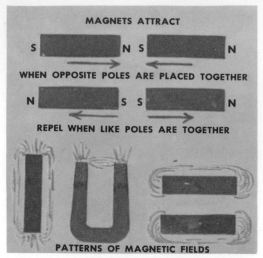

MAGNETS ATTRACT

WHEN OPPOSITE POLES ARE PLACED TOGETHER

REPEL WHEN LIKE POLES ARE TOGETHER

PATTERNS OF MAGNETIC FIELDS

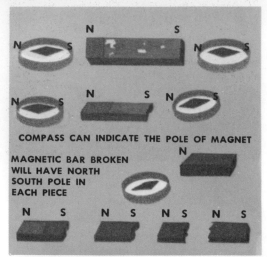

COMPASS CAN INDICATE THE POLE OF MAGNET

MAGNETIC BAR BROKEN WILL HAVE NORTH SOUTH POLE IN EACH PIECE

name "lodestone," (*leading stone*). The properties of magnetite were first investigated by the English physician, William Gilbert, whose famous treatise "De Magnete" appeared around the year 1600.

Experiments show that magnetism is not distributed evenly over the surface of a magnet. If a bar magnet or piece of lodestone is dipped into a pile of iron filings, the filings will cling in large clusters near the ends of the magnet. These end points are called the *poles* of the magnet. If a magnet is suspended like a COMPASS needle, the same end will always point in a northerly direction. This fact shows that the poles of the magnet are of two different types. This point is more clearly demonstrated if two like (such as both north) poles of magnets are brought together. The two like poles repel each other. If two unlike poles are brought together, there is a definite attraction between the two. Thus the familiar law is derived—*like poles repel and unlike poles attract.* In ordinary practice, the end of the magnet which seeks the north geographic pole is called a *north pole*, and the south-seeking end is called the *south pole*. They are also referred to as *positive and negative poles*.

Precise experiments show that the poles of a magnet have exactly the same strength even though they are of opposite sign. A north or south pole cannot exist by itself. If a bar magnet is cut into several pieces, new poles will be formed at each of the new ends, and each new piece will also have a north and south pole. However, the poles of an extremely long bar magnet will behave as if they are alone because the poles are so widely separated that neither pole affects the action of the other.

A magnet produces in the space around it a *magnetic field*. The field is strongest near the pole and becomes progressively weaker as the distance from the pole is increased. This effect can be shown quite simply by sprinkling iron filings on a sheet of paper and placing a magnet directly underneath the paper. A variety of combinations and patterns can be obtained with different types of magnets. Note that the filings arrange themselves in lines, and the strength of the pole is indicated by the density of their grouping around the magnet.

The fact that the filings do arrange themselves in lines is significant. These lines indicate the direction in which very small magnets would tend to lie if they were placed in the field of the large magnet. *A line of force* can be defined as a path in the field with a direction such that a magnet will always align itself parallel to the path.

The lines of iron filings are not themselves lines of force, but the filings lie along some of these lines of force. The relative spacing between the lines of force in any region is a measure of the strength of the magnetic field in that region.

Magnetism can be induced in a piece of ordinary iron or steel if it is placed near a very strong magnet. If a piece of steel is

A MAGNETIC FIELD IS A TOTAL EFFECT OF THE ROTATION OF ELECTRONS OF ATOMS OF A SUBSTANCE WHICH ARE IN ALIGNMENT

placed near a magnet and again iron filings are spread on a sheet of paper placed over the combination, the magnetic lines of force tend to go into the steel. Considering only the filings near the steel, they appear to emerge from the bar just as though it were itself a magnet. The steel bar has thus been magnetized by INDUCTION.

Assuming that a bar of steel is placed parallel to a magnet, the bar will have a south pole induced at the end which is next to the north pole of the magnet. Similarly, a north pole is induced in the end next to the magnet's south pole. The above is true regardless of which ends of the steel bar are placed next to the north and south poles of the magnet. This is interesting because the pole of a magnet will induce another pole of opposite sign.

Hence it is seen that repulsion is not possible between ordinary iron or steel and a permanent magnet. Repulsion is a property shown only by permanent magnets.

Some hint of the cause of magnetic properties is given by the fact that when a magnet is broken in two, it produces two new poles. If these parts are broken again and those parts are in turn broken, each new piece is a magnet. It is reasonable to assume, then, that if the pieces were broken into molecular size, each molecule of the material would be a magnet. This is called the *molecular theory of magnetism.*

According to the molecular theory, each tiny molecule is a magnet. When a piece of iron or steel is placed in a strong magnetic field, these molecules all become arranged in the same direction. Since they all have their north poles facing one end and the south poles facing the other, a large magnet is formed. Steel takes a stronger field to arrange these molecules than does soft iron,

and once they are arranged, it takes a stronger force to disarrange them. This explains the actions of soft iron cores found in ELECTROMAGNETS. A permanent magnet may be demagnetized by heating it to a dull red. The increased kinetic motion of the molecules at this temperature causes them to be disarranged and thus the magnetic effects of one molecule cancel those from another.

A more recent and probably more adequate theory attributes the property of magnetism to the motion of the electrons in their orbits. It is known that moving electrons really act as an electric current and that electric currents produce magnetic fields. (Electromagnets are an example of this.) It is thought that in certain atoms the spin-produced magnetic fields of the electrons are not completely balanced by the sum of all the magnetic fields of all electrons in the atom. If atoms of this type are put in a group, a surplus of uncompensated magnetic fields exists and all of these surplus fields acting together create the magnetic effects. The atoms of a number of common elements, such as aluminum and copper, do not contain enough surplus electron magnetic fields to make the material itself magnetic. A. E. L.

SEE ALSO: ELECTRICITY; ELECTRON; POLES, NORTH AND SOUTH

Magnetic pole see Compass; Poles, North and South

Magnetite (MAGG-nuh-tite) Most magnetic bodies must be made magnetic by using some outside influence such as electricity. There are, however, certain metals which naturally possess the ability to attract other metals. These natural magnets, called *lodestones,* are composed of an iron oxide called *magnetite.*

Generally, magnetite is found in the unmagnetized state. Even in the unmagnetized state it is still much more strongly attracted by other magnets than most metals. Another common name for this iron ore is *magnetic iron.* The chemical composition of magnetite is Fe_3O_4. It has a specific gravity of 5.18 and its hardness is six on the Mohs HARDNESS SCALE. A. E. L.

SEE ALSO: EMERY, HEMATITE, IRON

Young People's
Science Encyclopedia

YOUNG PEOPLE'S
SCIENCE ENCYCLOPEDIA

Edited by the Staff of
NATIONAL COLLEGE OF EDUCATION, Evanston, Ill.

ASSOCIATE EDITORS

HELEN J. CHALLAND, B.E., M.A., Ph.D.
Chairman, Science-Mathematics
Department
National College of Education

DONALD A. BOYER, B.S., M.S., Ph.D.
Science Education Consultant, Winnetka
Public Schools, Winnetka, Ill.
Science, National College of Education

EDITORIAL CONSULTANTS
ON THE STAFF OF NATIONAL COLLEGE OF EDUCATION

Elizabeth R. Brandt, B.A., M.Ed.
Eugene B. Cantelupe, B.A., M.F.A., Ph.D.
John H. Daugherty, B.S., M.A.
Irwin K. Feinstein, B.S., M.A., Ph.D.
Mary Gallagher, A.B., M.A., Ph.D.
Beatrice S. Garber, A.B., M.S., Ph.D.

Hal S. Galbreath, B.S. Ed., M.S.
Robert R. Kidder, A.B., M.A., Ph.D.
Jean C. Kraft, B.S., M.A., Ph.D.
Elise P. Lerman, B.A., B.F.A., M.F.A.
Mary-Louise Neumann, A.B., B.S.L.S.
Lavon Rasco, B.A., M.A., Ph.D.

Bruce Allen Thale, B.S.Ed., M.S.Ed.

SPECIAL SUBJECT AREA CONSULTANTS

Krafft A. Ehricke, B.A.E., H.L.D.
Benjamin M. Hair, A.B., M.D.
Charles B. Johnson, B.S., M.A., M.S.

H. Kenneth Scatliff, M.D.
Ray C. Soliday, B.A., B.S., M.A. (Deceased)
Fred R. Wilkin, Jr., B.A., M.Ed.

Raymond J. Johnson, B.B.A., M.Ed.

THE STAFF

Project Editor	Frances Dyra
Assistant Editor	Elizabeth Rhein
Editorial Assistants	Helen Patton Smith, Barbara Ayukawa, Judith Chaffin
Editorial Production Assistant	Shirley Labieniec
Production Manager	Nelson McAllister
Production Assistants	John Andrews, Mitzi Trout